# BREAD, CEMENT, CACTUS

In this exploration of the meaning of home, Annie Zaidi reflects on the places in India from which she derives her sense of identity. She looks back on the now renamed city of her birth and the impossibility of belonging in the industrial township where she grew up. From her ancestral village, in a region notorious for its gangsters, to the mega-city where she now lives, Zaidi provides a nuanced perspective on forging a sense of belonging as a minority and a migrant in places where other communities consider you an outsider, and of the fragility of home left behind and changed beyond recognition. Zaidi is the 2019/2020 winner of the Nine Dots Prize, which seeks to reward creative thinking that tackles contemporary social issues. This book is also available as Open Access.

Annie Zaidi is a freelance journalist and scriptwriter based in Mumbai, India, and was named by *Elle* magazine as one of the emerging South Asian writers 'whose writing ... will enrich South Asian literature'. Her first novel, *Prelude to a Riot*, was published in 2019. Other books include *Known Turf: Bantering with Bandits and Other True Tales*, a collection of essays based on her experiences as a reporter, which was shortlisted for the Crossword Book Award in 2010, and *Love Stories # 1 to 14*, a collection of short fiction published in 2012. She also edited the anthology *Unbound: 2,000 Years of Indian Women's Writing*, published in 2015.

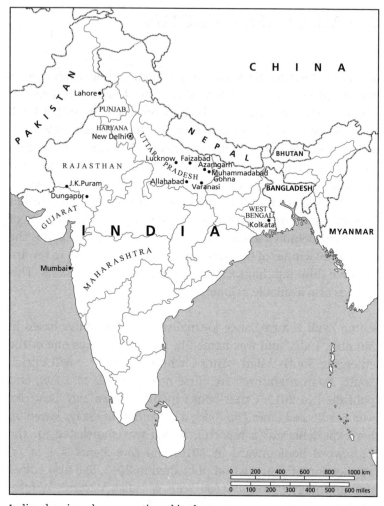

India, showing places mentioned in the text.

# ANNIE ZAIDI

# BREAD

*A Memoir*

# CEMENT

*of Belonging and Dislocation*

# CACTUS

With original illustrations by Yasmin Zaidi

CAMBRIDGE
UNIVERSITY PRESS

# CAMBRIDGE
UNIVERSITY PRESS

University Printing House, Cambridge CB2 8BS, United Kingdom

One Liberty Plaza, 20th Floor, New York, NY 10006, USA

477 Williamstown Road, Port Melbourne, VIC 3207, Australia

314–321, 3rd Floor, Plot 3, Splendor Forum, Jasola District Centre,
New Delhi – 110025, India

79 Anson Road, #06–04/06, Singapore 079906

Cambridge University Press is part of the University of Cambridge.

It furthers the University's mission by disseminating knowledge in the pursuit of
education, learning, and research at the highest international levels of excellence.

www.cambridge.org
Information on this title: www.cambridge.org/9781108840644
DOI: 10.1017/9781108886932

First published 2020

Printed in the United Kingdom by TJ International Ltd, Padstow Cornwall

A catalogue record for this publication is available from the British Library.

ISBN 978-1-108-84064-4 Hardback
ISBN 978-1-108-81463-8 Paperback

# CONTENTS

# ABOUT THE NINE DOTS PRIZE

The Nine Dots Prize was established to promote innovative thinking as a means of tackling pressing problems facing the modern world. Its name, which comes from the lateral-thinking nine dots puzzle, sums up what we were hoping it would result in – outside-of-the-box responses to the biggest issues of the day.

In 2018, for the second cycle of the prize, we asked the question 'Is there still no place like home?'

The prize was judged anonymously, as always, with the Board selecting its winner based solely on their 3,000-word essay. As a result, new writers jostle with experienced authors, and submissions have come from people of all backgrounds with one shared ambition: to develop their ideas into a full-length book.

We were delighted by the several hundred submissions we received and the vast number of different ways each dealt with the question we posed. Despite having proven herself already as a journalist and a fiction writer, it was an honour to be able to give our winner, Annie Zaidi, an international platform fully to explore the ideas of home and belonging about which she is so passionate. Annie had been thinking about a project along the lines of *Bread, Cement, Cactus* for some time. We are proud that the Nine Dots Prize has provided her with the opportunity to do her vision justice.

It is our hope that once the book is published, Annie's ideas will find a wide readership and prompt ongoing debate. Hers is a powerful and compelling voice with a unique insight into what home means for citizens of the world today.

Annie follows in the footsteps of our inaugural winner, James Williams, a former Google strategist turned Oxford student and philosopher, whose book, *Stand Out of Our Light: Freedom and*

*Resistance in the Attention Economy,* was a warning on the societal impact of the attention economy and the political power held by just a few major tech firms. Published in May 2018, it received critical acclaim ('A landmark book' – the *Observer*; 'Switch off your smartphone, slouch in a comfy chair, and pay your full, undivided, attention to this short, absorbing, and deeply disturbing book' – *Financial Times*). While their subjects, backgrounds and expertise differ dramatically, Annie and James share a commitment to finding new ways of looking at important societal questions. It is in that spirit that the Nine Dots Prize was established.

We hope you will continue to follow the Prize, as we seek to ignite new discussions on the issues that affect us all.

Professor Simon Goldhill
*Director of the Centre for Research in the Arts, Social Sciences and Humanities (CRAASH) at Cambridge University and Chair of the Nine Dots Prize Board*

For more about the Nine Dots Prize please visit ninedotsprize.org

I needed to see it written in black and white, up on a wall.

جہاں کوئی اپنا دفن نہ ہوا ہو وہ جگہ اپنی نہیں ہوا کرتی

*Jahan koyi apna dafn na hua ho woh jagah apni nahin hua karti*

Travelling from Spanish to English to Urdu with its curlicue graces, that line waited to trip me up in my own language. I found it at a stall selling posters at a literary festival. It's from Gabriel Garcia Marquez' *One Hundred Years of Solitude*: A person does not belong to a place until someone beloved is buried there.

In north India, where my family is from, a corpse is sometimes referred to as *mitti*. Soil. Earth, if you prefer, and when you want to emphasise your relationship with the land, you might declare, '*Yahaan meri purkhon ki naal garhi hai*', 'This is where my ancestor's umbilical cord is buried'.

I must have come upon this sentence about burying beloveds when I first read Marquez, but it hadn't leapt off the page then. I hadn't buried anyone yet. I hadn't even been inside a graveyard. I hadn't yet been told that I didn't belong in my own country, or that I had a smaller right to it. Belonging, however, had always been a fraught question for me. Friends from journalism school continue to tease me about the first day of class when a professor asked us to introduce ourselves: just names and where we're from. I said I wasn't sure where I was from, and then proceeded to list everywhere I'd lived thus far.

What I was trying to say was that I felt dislocated, and anxious about my fractured identity. I was born in a hospital and I don't know if my cord was buried at all. I'd never lived in the city of my birth and only briefly in the city where my grandparents lived. Leaving us with her parents while she went back to university, my mother quit a bad marriage. Later, she found a job and moved with her two children to a remote industrial township in Rajasthan. The need for bread, and milk for the children, overrode her unease at being so far from everything familiar.

We rarely had much choice about moving. Four walls and a roof don't do much good if there's no bread on the table. So we moved. Thoughts about how we *felt* about where we lived were an indulgence we couldn't afford.

Now here I was, staring at funky literary memorabilia, thinking about what I'd do with myself when I was my mother's age.

I bought that Marquez poster and took it to the framer's. For a moment, I stood hesitating. Framing would prolong the paper's life. On the other hand, a glass and wood frame might be damaged in transit. Transit, at any rate, was inevitable.

JK Puram is an industrial township in Rajasthan, flanked by the Aravalli hills and a cement factory.

# 1  SURVIVORS SHALL BE PROSECUTED

One of my first memories of the place is cactus. Another is playing in piles of sieved sand that was waiting to be mixed into concrete.

The *colony*, a word often used to describe industrial townships and urban residential complexes in India, was dry and dusty. Summer temperatures inched towards fifty degrees centigrade. It was flanked on one side by the Aravalli hills, one of the oldest hill ranges in the world. On the other side stood a cement factory.

Everyone in this colony knew their place. Houses were allotted on the basis of jobs held at the factory. 'A' type quarters were for top management. These were spacious bungalows with a lawn and the services of a gardener. Upper management lived in 'B' type, middle management in 'C' type, blue-collar workers in 'E' and 'F' type. We were in 'D' type, meant for those who were not quite managers but couldn't be classified as 'workers' either. People like my mother. She was vice-principal and later principal at a school meant for the children of factory employees.

The children of managers and furnace stokers attended the same school, but even 6-year-olds know how A-B-C-D goes. 'D' type was a cramped two-bedroom house with vertical iron bars on windows, doors of hewn planks, and concrete everywhere including the bathroom floor. No marble, no glass, no tiles, no garden. After my mother was promoted, one of my E-type friends had asked, 'I suppose you'll be hanging out with the C-type girls now?'

I didn't know at the time that there was a 'W' and an 'LC' too, quarters for watchmen and loaders respectively. I didn't see those quarters in the eleven years I spent there.

The roads were pure concrete – cement was one thing the township didn't lack – but traffic was almost non-existent. Only top management had cars; a few of the men rode scooters. Most of us just walked. Besides, there wasn't anywhere to go. No movie theatre, no restaurant, no shopping except for basic groceries, no café, no parks, no pools, no bookstore, no buses, no taxis.

If you needed to go out of the colony, you had to fill in a requisition form to ask for a car and driver. The district head-quarters, Sirohi, was an hour's drive. It had a hospital where I was once admitted after a serious fracture and where I almost lost the use of a leg. It also had tailors' shops and bakeries. The cakes that mysteriously showed up on my birthday were made there. It had a railway station where, twice a year, we boarded a train to go visit my grandparents.

If you were desperate to escape without actually leaving the colony, your only recourse was the Aravalli hills. Ancient, stoic and never fully colonised, the hills were the reason the cement factory existed. Limestone deposits were torn out with explosives, and we were warned not to go climbing when a blast was scheduled. We never got to see the dynamite but we did hear the periodic *boom!* in the distance.

We'd climb the hill nearest the colony, sometimes with a sandwich picnic. Once there, we scratched our names on flat rocks with sharp-edged flint. Seeing my name, white on bluish-grey rock, brought cheap satisfaction: here I am, alive, but at risk of death by boredom.

We were warned not to climb the hills that couldn't be seen from the colony. There were stories about Bhīl tribesmen who lived there and who could relieve kids of their valuables. We'd heard of petty theft in the colony – clothes taken off clotheslines, jars of clarified butter stolen from kitchens – and out on the highway, of robberies conducted after boulders were nudged off the slope onto approaching vehicles.

I wasn't sure I believed the stories. Still, I didn't want to venture beyond the first row of hills. Scarier than being accosted and having my earrings taken away was the landscape itself: hill behind hill and beyond that, more hill. Not a soul in sight.

In the colony, everything revolved around the factory. Sirens summoned workers to their respective shifts, and we'd see them hurrying to work. Once in a while, a truck loaded with cement would rumble past.

Everyone I knew was an outsider who needed a job; everyone left as soon as a better opportunity presented itself. No outsiders were allowed in unless they were employees or their guests. The colony was gated and guarded. We never mixed with the children of farmers or shepherds who lived in villages barely a couple of kilometres away.

A township like this was a set of tasks and norms. It fed you but it didn't ground you. You couldn't, even if you wanted to, buy property here. Even if you were the sort of person who adored life in an industrial township, you couldn't stake a claim to it. On the other hand, those who did own land around here were near invisible. Nobody ever talked about what, or who, was here before the factory was built. I grew up with a sense that there was nothing before, and it wasn't hard to believe. There was enough cactus and acacia around to suggest a desert. Yet, there were fields of corn, sheep, cattle, a few camels.

We had glimpses of men in white dhotis and turbans, women in bright skirts. When a new building for the school was to be constructed, or a road had to be extended, they'd show up and I'd stare in wonder. Girls with distinctive tattoos and rows of metallic hairpins, men with earrings and tie-front shirts. Slowly, I learnt to tell the tribes apart – Garāsia, Rabādi, Bhīl.

The Rabādi were traditionally animal herders and they supplied us with milk. The Garāsia were farmers who came to work in the colony as wage labourers. Their children did not attend the school, though some teenagers came to work as domestic helps in the homes of colony residents. We didn't know how far they walked to get to the colony. None of us knew their languages. Their languages were not even recognised as such by the state. The factory, the school and living quarters of every 'type' had been constructed by the tribes who lived in surrounding villages.

*

Very few people have heard of JK Puram unless they had jobs here or family members were employees. Most people outside the state haven't even heard of Sirohi, the district in which the township is located.

Our nearest point of reference was Mount Abu, a 'hill station' that had once been used as a regional administrative centre by the British government and is now an affordable honeymoon destination in western India.

Mount Abu was where we would go for school picnics and field trips, and to write our final high school examinations. It was full of pretty picnic spots, but my favourite place was Trevor's Tank on account of its warning sign: SWIMMING STRICTLY PROHIBITED. SURVIVORS SHALL BE PROSECUTED.

I used to think it was hilarious: to survive only to be prosecuted. I was too young to know what people did – or were willing to do – to survive. I didn't fully understand private property or what legislating water or land meant. I did know that prosecution meant being hauled off by the police, and perhaps jailed. I didn't know what jail meant except what I saw in movies – it was a place where everyone wore uniforms and always wanted to escape.

I wanted to escape JK Puram and its sameness, its siren rhythms, the prickly things it concealed.

Twenty years passed before I returned to look at it with grown-up eyes. To speak with those who were here *before* and who would stay if the factory were to shut down. What was their relationship with outsiders who profited from the landscape that they traditionally saw as their own?

In Basantgarh village, I was introduced to Vaghta Ram. He listened intently while another activist explained my quest in the Garāsia language, then he thrust out his hands, which were covered in cement, and began to speak agitatedly. I had to interrupt: Hindi please.

He switched to Hindi. 'These hands built that place. All the old buildings, the factory, the—'

Slow down, I had to say. Begin at the beginning. In the beginning, he told me, about twenty Garāsia families lived on the land that became JK Puram. They farmed approximately 150 bighas collectively. There is no standard measure for a bigha in south Asia, but it could be anything between one third of an acre to one acre.[1]

Younger men had gathered around by now. Someone piped up, 'It was a thousand bighas!' Vaghta Ram shut him up firmly. I will not tell lies, he said, it was about 150 bighas.

It was not a place utterly devoid of state institutions or facilities. He is about 70 years old now and remembers that there was a government school in the village when he was a child. He was educated up to the eighth grade though classes were run under a tree, open to the sky, for the first five years. In the early 1970s, when he was in his mid twenties, land was acquired for a new factory and as part of the acquisition deal, the company promised to hire one man from each family as a permanent employee. The land was taken at nominal prices because in those days none of them knew what it was worth. They also didn't know that this place had been chosen because of its limestone deposits.

Vaghta Ram can account for thirteen men who got jobs, mostly in the packing or mining departments. He himself worked as a labour contractor and construction worker for twenty odd years, earning as little as 5 rupees as a daily wage at first. The *kārigar* (mason) earned the most: 9 rupees. Over the years, wages rose. But one thing remained constant – none of the Basantgarh workers were assigned living quarters inside the colony. Housing, they were told, was for those who needed it, which was outsiders. Workers from the surrounding villages walked between 2 and 5 kilometres each way. Kids whose fathers were not employed at the factory were not admitted to the colony school.

Resentment was slow to set in, but it had set in now. A young man, Praveen Singh Rao, cut into the conversation. His own father and uncle, he said, were due to retire in 2019. They were among the handful of men hired as 'permanent' employees. But Praveen could not attend the school my mother worked at – a better school, after all, which offered an English medium education – because it was too far for a child to walk. Sacrifices were made eventually, for the sake of his younger siblings. The family rented rooms sublet by another employee, who had been allotted a colony house since he lived further away, but who owned a vehicle and didn't mind the commute.

The richer a man was, the more assets he possessed, the more money he stands to make, and the better educated his kids are, no matter his proximity to the workplace. Learning this lesson has angered Praveen. There are other resentments. Blasting for limestone in the hillside causes cracks in the walls of the homes of villagers. A dam has been built across the West Banas River, and it supplies plentiful water to the industrial township. It does not irrigate the fields of farmers. For their own drinking and basic household needs, the village has to buy water supplied by private individuals in tankers.

Vaghta Ram said he stopped working for the JK Group after one of his nephews fell to his death while working on a construction site. He filed a suit demanding compensation, but lost the case. He never wanted to work for the company again. That his hands are covered in cement now is on account of building something in his own village. He has a bit of land and he grows millets and corn.

I asked if farming wasn't harder work, with no guarantee of a good rain or a decent harvest? It is harder, he said, yet he feels more in control. On his own land, he isn't taking orders from another man. He is, however, of the old guard. Young men like Praveen are angry that a younger, better educated generation is not getting hired at the factory. Forty years have passed and Basantgarh sends no managers or engineers to JK Puram. Young people are not offered internships if they sign up for technical or engineering courses. Even girls are going to college now, including Vaghta Ram's daughters, but they aren't getting hired in the colony, which seeks only 'workers'.

Even in the worker category, there is little hope of secure employment. Several departments have been outsourced by the manufacturer-industrialists to subcontractors. Jobs in construction, packing and loading are now going to labourers brought here from other states.

Is the 'outsider' labour much cheaper? I asked. No, I'm told. But outsiders are unlikely to organise, or expect anything bar wages. If they lose jobs, they are unlikely to make a fuss. They go home quietly.

Basantgarh is one of the villages 'adopted' by the industrial township. Relative to other Adivasi villages, more concrete is in evidence. There is no functional hospital with emergency facilities. The local health centre built by the government has an attendant nurse, but there is no resident doctor. This centre was locked when I visited, in the middle of a weekday afternoon. Occasionally the JK Group sends around a van with doctors, the villagers admit as much. However, these are not services people can rely on, or take for granted. The JK Puram school also admits children of non-employees now, but it is not free, nor so heavily subsidised as to benefit the poorest tribespeople.

The village is entitled to a limestone mining royalty and a small share of cement. The villagers agree, it *is* substantial money, but they allege that it gets cornered by the *panchayat* (village council) head. The last man who controlled the council also happened to be a union leader at the cement factory. He also happened to be a Rajput, not Garāsia. Nobody would say directly how the funds were used. Ask the factory people, some of the younger men said. Ask, how that man roams about in such an expensive car; how he can build a hotel where, it is rumoured, a cup of tea is going to cost 300 rupees? Ask, who pays for the fuel in his car?

I asked a different question: why did that man get elected when this village has a majority of Garāsia people? Nobody answered.

*

The story of losing power, then losing ground, is not a new one. In *Rajasthan: A Concise History*, Rima Hooja writes that a common motif in the founding narratives of many former kingdoms is Rajput warriors seizing power from forest- and hill-dwelling tribes. Folk tales and genealogies describe the overthrow of indigenous chiefs by Kshtriyas (ranked second highest in the Hindu caste hierarchy), who entered unfamiliar tracts either as refugees or invaders. To reassert sovereignty, and perhaps to affirm the loyalty of the tribes they conquered, kingdoms like Mewār and Dungarpur held coronation rituals where a Bhīl representative anointed the forehead of the Rajput successor.

Each kingdom had dozens of *thikānās*, fiefs controlled by Rajput feudal lords. Having lost their sovereignty, tribal communities now had to pay crushing revenues and dozens of additional taxes. They also had to perform forced labour, a practice called *begār*, and serve on hunting expeditions, for which they were not compensated. In some thikānās, they were also beaten for the smallest sign of intransigence, even if the intransigence had been enacted by the animals that were being hunted.[2]

At various times, the tribes resisted. In 1839, Bhīl and Garāsia tribesmen killed some soldiers of the kingdom of Mewār, which led to the ruler setting up a military garrison to keep them in check. Sirohi, having signed a treaty with the British East India Company, also put down rebellions by Bhīls and Mīnas.

After a devastating famine at the turn of the last century, a tribal leader called Guru Govindgiri (originally Govinda Gobpalia) had emerged as a voice of resistance, but he was arrested and exiled, and very narrowly escaped the death penalty. Govindgiri had had a vision for the restoration of an indigenous kingdom – a Bhīl Raj – though he couldn't quite envision cultural autonomy. He spoke out against forced labour and taxes but also wanted his followers to give up meat and alcohol, which ran counter to Bhīl and Garāsiya culture. Other activists, too, were intent on the 'upliftment' of tribes and the 'modernisation' of their 'negative' lifestyle.[3]

Non-tribal, non-forest communities looked down upon tribespeople who lived by hunting, gathering forest produce, and practising a shifting form of cultivation. The administration also disapproved, partly because mobile groups couldn't be taxed very easily. After the early twentieth-century Land Revenue Settlement in princely states like Dungarpur, Sirohi and Banswara, the traditional rights of the tribes were further curtailed: shifting cultivation was forbidden, and access to honey, bamboo and other forest produce was cut off.[4] Political resistance was crushed, often brutally.

Matters reached a head in 1920, with the 'Akki' or 'Eki' movement being suppressed by local rulers, British troops assisting. In May 1922, between 1,200 and 1,500 tribespeople were killed. Among the villages that were set ablaze was the village of Bhula in Sirohi.

*

When I texted him, asking to meet, he responded with his address and name drawn out to reflect a political consciousness of his identity: Mukesh Gameti Bhīl Adivasi.

He is, he says, the only man of his tribe from his village, Bhula, who has tackled competition. He uses 'competition' in the sense of taking exams that lead to government jobs. Going to college, travelling, paying fees – these are beyond the reach of most people in his community. He managed to graduate and land a job teaching at a government secondary school.

A lot has changed since the 1980s. For one, there are social networks and the Bhīl are starting to organise themselves. Mukesh is keenly aware of the movement for greater autonomy, spearheaded by the Bhil Autonomous Council, and the international recognition of indigenous rights. He is also aware of the political dependence of his people.

Bhīls, along with Mīnas, Garāsias, Sahariyas and several other indigenous tribes, are recognised as such by the Constitution of India and referred to as 'scheduled tribes', abbreviated to ST in common parlance. Electoral seats are reserved for them in state assemblies and in Parliament. Yet their interests, particularly the right to forest produce and water, are not safeguarded. Mukesh admits, representatives are often propped up by 'third parties', which is to say, larger political organisations. Whenever there is a conflict of interests, ST interests are betrayed.

I told him about growing up hearing stories about the Bhīl on the other side of the hill, waiting to accost me and divest me of my earrings. He grinned. Bhula, he said, was once known to be a dangerous place. The people of his tribe who lived in the hills beyond JK Puram didn't lose farmland during the setting up of the township. What they did lose is impossible to articulate.

I asked Mukesh to try. He said, he'd heard that the land around the mining area was starting to turn barren. But there are no independent studies on environmental impact, no soil pollution data one could cite. Using the Right to Information, a law enacted in 2005, Mukesh wrote to the district magistrate, seeking information about the renewal of mining leases, royalties on limestone extraction, and whether 10 per cent of all permanent jobs were indeed reserved for local residents. He asked for a list of people who had those jobs. He got a reply telling him to seek the information from other departments.

Jobs were a flint that set off sparks of heat in every conversation. Strike enough times, and it comes back to the question of natural resources. Communities that were once dependent only on nature had to submit to others who took control of these resources, and this dependence is an uncertain one.

There are two labour unions now at the factory, where once there was only one. Both have relationships with major political parties. Neither has managed to secure more jobs for local residents. The JK Lakshmi Cement website has a sustainability tab. The 2014–16 report mentions initiatives aimed at maternal health awareness across thirty-five villages, and education programmes for differently abled children.[5] But it does not mention how many jobs the factory can sustain. It does not offer data on the rate of employee hire by subcontractors or the gender profile of the workforce.

A scion of the family after whom the cement brand is named, Lakshmipat Singhania, is quoted in the report as saying: 'We seek a society which is proud of its past, conscious of the present and full of hope for the future.'

The infographic below shows buildings in green hues, with solar panels, a human figure leaning to construct something, another figure putting litter in a bin, a bicycle. I was visiting the colony after twenty years, and saw few bicycles. There were more cars, although everything in the township is still within walking distance. I did see solar panels. The report mentioned that the company was getting into the business of renewable energy. It mentioned greenhouse gas and carbon emissions but said nothing about the environmental impact of blasting the ancient Aravalli hills for limestone.

There is another quote from one of the ancient spiritual texts, the Ishvasya Upanishad. It says: 'find your enjoyment in renunciation, do not covet what belongs to others'.

What belongs to whom? What, and how much, can be taken from nature? Who pays the costs of what is taken and cannot be returned? Tricky questions. To answer would mean to admit that belonging and coveting have to be seen through historical prisms, for it is history that informs narratives about what is ours to take, and what is not.

The rocks in the Aravalli hills near Sirohi are over 1,400 million years old. According to a 1981 census, the Adivasi or ST population in this district was over 23 per cent (it is now over 28 per cent). JK Lakshmi Cement was set up in 1982. According to the company's website, it boasts a turnover of 30 billion Indian rupees (418 million USD) and produces 13.30 million tonnes of cement a year.

The state, Rajasthan, leads on cement production, with limestone deposits in twenty-five of its thirty-three districts. Twenty-three cement factories already exist.[6] The limestone mining lease issued to JK Lakshmi Cement led to jobs for 204 people.[7] We could assume that all of these jobs went to residents of the surrounding villages, though that would not necessarily be an accurate assumption.

What has been taken then, in lieu of what?

\*

Cactus remains entwined with my feeling for the place. One thorny memory is waking up to an undercurrent of violence beneath the sameness of life, with adults muttering about 'union' and 'strike'. On such days, we were sent home from school and told to be careful, not to loiter outdoors. Nobody explained, but the fence between 'worker' and 'management' was suddenly explicit.

Returning after two decades, I asked some of the older school-teachers if they remembered such days. They did. One recalled having to escort the smaller children home, and added things were somewhat worse now. I asked why. She said, 'they' used bows and arrows to threaten the management before. Now there are guns.

The 'they' is undefined. It goes without saying that those who brandished bows and arrows were those who knew how to use them. What is not so clear is whether they brandished these arms in their own interest, for they have clearly not gained the upper hand.

Perhaps it is not so odd, after all, that an industrial township should be called a 'colony'. It is not a town that has sprung up organically, in response to the needs of those who live there. Factories usually make profits for outsiders who live elsewhere, speak other languages, are likely to bury or scatter the ashes of their beloveds elsewhere. This, at least, they have in common with systems that render entire nations 'colonies'.

Those who worked in JK Puram as managers over the last few decades didn't need to learn the language of the Adivasis. They would not have known the tribes' ballads, or the logic of their marital customs. They came as outsiders, and left culturally unchallenged. It was the Adivasis who had to adapt, learning Hindi and English. I could talk to them without an interpreter. They did not refuse to talk to me, but there was little doubt in either of our minds that I came speaking the language of power, and that the balance of power was tilted against them.

I wonder what it might have been like if the dreams of early twentieth-century activists had been realised: what if the factory was located in a Bhīl Raj, or a Garāsiya Raj?

Would we study Bheeli as a first or second language in schools? Would we have committed to a different strand of collective memory: singing paeans to Adivasi heroes, absorbing their aesthetic, learning skills like hunting, sculpting and farming?

There are fresh attempts at reclaiming indigenous territories. A political outfit called the Bharatiya Tribal Party won two seats in the 2018 state assembly elections. It is demanding a separate state made up of lands that have a significant Bhīl population. One of its leaders pointed out in an interview that a distinct political 'state' is crucial for the preservation of cultural identity, which some activists are trying to erode.[8] Despite being Bhīl themselves, they want their people to 'imitate the general population'.

Bhīl and Garāsiya culture *is* different from the 'general' or, more specifically, upper-caste norm. This reflects not only in body language but in emotional and sexual practices.

As a teenager, I used to watch the girls who came to work in the colony with a mix of fascination and nervousness. Their skirts took in several yards of fabric and their *odhnis* (a type of sari) were used more as practical scarves/sun shields than as an aide to modesty. They wore tattoos, sometimes their own names stamped on their forearms. On hot summer afternoons, they would push long blouses up so the breeze could touch their bellies and backs. The girls laughed easily, and even as a child, I saw that the way they walked, talked, looked at others was less inhibited than peers in the 'general' population.

Occasionally, an Adivasi girl who worked in someone's home would disappear. We heard whispers about the girl having eloped. To non-tribal girls, this was an incredible act, a source of undying shame. But a few months later, the girl would reappear, clearly unashamed. Sometimes we'd hear that a girl had left the man she'd eloped with. The gossip was accompanied by tut-tutting on the part of colony aunties and comments like, 'These things happen among these people.'

I caught a note of distress along with contempt, but was too young to know of cultural wars. 'These people' were indigenous or 'mool nivasi', as they are officially acknowledged to be, the earliest inhabitants of the land. Tut-tutting aunties were groomed to see upper-caste marital practices as the norm, where marriage was arranged and divorce forbidden, and any deviation was punished through social ostracism. To see the norm challenged so easily, to see that it caused no significant damage to the girls, was distressing to them.

Among many tribes in India, there is a tradition of bride price rather than dowry. Therefore, there is a tradition of elopements among young couples if the boy cannot negotiate a price that meets expectations. There is also a tradition of living together without performing wedding rituals, which continues to raise brows. The Hindi press tends to write headlines such as 'Live-in . . . a Jaw-dropping news about the tribes' (sic).[9]

The Adivasi leadership wants no mainstreaming. What it wants is water access, rights over natural wealth such as minerals and marble, and preventing 'outsiders' from buying Adivasi lands.[10]

This is a common demand by tribes in hill and forested areas. Laws have been framed in some states that limit the right of Indian citizens' to acquire land unless they can prove local residency for a certain number of years. This is partly to protect the rights of the poor, who may not know the market value of their lands, partly to ensure that the demographic does not change suddenly. Perhaps there is an additional concern about land being controlled by those who are not deeply invested in the local ecology and economy.

The rules are frequently relaxed for politicians, religious organisations and industrial houses, of course. In fact, the government steps in to acquire land on behalf of industrialists and protests are overcome with the help of police or the armed forces. Often this ends with the killing or the jailing of activists and local leaders.

*

Emblazoned in giant white letters across the bosom of a hill that overlooks the colony is its name: JAY KAY PURAM. It can be seen from the windows of trains that chug through the area.

Seeing the name was exciting to the child who lived there. Looking at it with adult eyes, it seemed to have been planted like a flag of dominion. The initials 'J' and 'K' stand for Juggilal and Kamlapat Singhania, the founders of a business house that works in several sectors, including cement and tyre manufacture. For the sake of cement manufacture, the hills had to be blasted, limestone extracted. Rivers would supply water. Ground water would be extracted too. Perhaps it was necessary that the place be named for those who controlled not just the land but its resources.

Living under the shadow of that name, I had not interrogated such controls over nature and mineral. I started doing so only after I met communities that had been stripped of all the things that sheltered and nourished them – food, herbs, wood, water, cultural autonomy. On one assignment, I was on a bus with a group of activists on a journey to campaign for a law that granted citizens the right to work. The bus went through Rajasthan, north to south.

I was on familiar ground, and yet nothing seemed familiar. Adivasis, their concerns and goals, were different from those of the industrial township residents. At one public meeting, women began to speak about what it meant to not own land. It was not just the lack of a field to till, or a square upon which to build a house; it was also about not having anywhere to squat and shit without the fear of being attacked. It is impossible to live without fear on a daily basis, without land and water rights.

In 1927, the British passed a law bringing forests under the direct control of the government. This law has remained in force in India, and those who live in forests are considered encroachers unless they can prove otherwise. Since independence, around 50 million Indians have been displaced to make way for dams, industrial projects, highways and protected forest reserves.[11] The majority of the displaced, over 40 per cent, were Adivasis, who comprise only 8 per cent of the population.[12] If they refused to go quietly, they were evicted through brute measures including the use of elephants to knock down huts; their crops were destroyed and their homes set on fire by the state's paramilitary forces.[13]

Adivasis have tried to insist upon their right to stay within forests or to resist mining operations. There have been arrests and gunfire. One of the rare times a community did win a battle against an industrial giant, it was by insisting that the mountain was sacred; it could not be destroyed because it interfered with religion. Speaking of their right to live where their forefathers have always lived was not an acceptable argument. That just got them charged with rioting and other crimes.[14]

The Supreme Court of India has reaffirmed the state's right to evict over a million Adivasis living in forests, although studies indicate that forest dwelling communities find it hard to survive if separated from their traditional ways of life. To be removed from the forest is to be sentenced to a lack of bread and meat, fruit and flower, wine and wood.

Studies also indicate that rehabilitation rarely works – to be given a piece of land in a new location in return for access to a forest and community networks is a bargain so skewed, it is hard to enumerate. What can be enumerated is poverty and wealth. A study jointly undertaken by the Savitribai Phule Pune University, Jawaharlal Nehru University and the Indian Institute of Dalit Studies has found that a little over 22 per cent of India's upper-caste Hindus own 41 per cent of the country's wealth while the 7.8 per cent that comprise the scheduled tribes own just 3.7 per cent. The wealthiest 1 per cent own 25 per cent of the country's total assets, including land, while the bottom 40 per cent of households own just 3.4 per cent.[15]

Adivasis, displaced often, end up in cities where they are reduced to penury and homelessness. A recent study of fifteen cities across five Indian states has found that scheduled castes make up the largest proportion of the urban homeless, at 36 per cent, followed by scheduled tribes, who comprise 23 per cent. Worse, it isn't a temporary phase. Sixty per cent of the surveyed homeless had been born in the same city, which means their parents were possibly homeless too.[16]

Yet another study indicates that 50 per cent of India's Adivasi population is poor based on every indicator, including nutrition, health, education, living standards and ownership of assets.[17] So poor that some families in Rajasthan have ended up mortgaging children.[18] And what are the chances a mortgaged child can find a way to come back home?

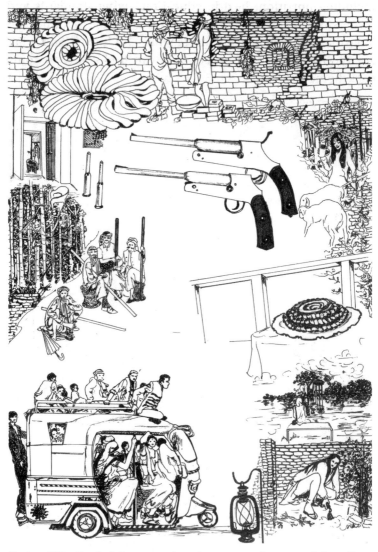

Eastern Uttar Pradesh is as notorious for goons and gangs as it is well known for its sugar industry.

# 2 GUR, IMARTI, GOONS

Growing up, I never knew how to answer questions about where I was from. I couldn't very well say, I'm from a dusty industrial township that I never want to see again. For the sake of convenience, I said, Lucknow. It was the city where we spent vacations, with family, but we don't have roots there.

Mom says our roots lie in Muhammadabad Gohna, a mofussil *kasba*, a village struggling to turn into a town. It used to be part of Azamgarh district once and is now in a new district called Mau. A few kilometres away is the village of Karhan, my grandfather's *nanihāl* (maternal ancestral home). We can trace back fourteen generations here. The uncle who told me this is now gone. Fifteen generations, then.

We are obvious misfits here. The women of the family rarely step outside for grocery, errands, or jobs. A new generation of girls does go to college, but they wear hijabs and burqas.

I fight with my mother: *We* don't come from *this*! *You* came from cities like Lucknow and Delhi, from secularism and cosmopolitanism, from an English-medium education. *You* wore breeches and rode horses!

Mom counters: *Daddy* said never to forget our *roots*. Over all protest, she builds a morsel-sized house there. Within the walls of a large ancestral house, several branches of the family have built individual units. It wears a deserted look around the year, but comes alive during the month of Moharram. Shia families across the state return to ancestral homes, especially for the first ten days, to mark the tragedy within which all tragedies are meant to be subsumed – the martyrdom of Imam Hussain and the slaughter and devastation that visited his clan in Karbala. Individual grief is folded into an unending sorrow that connects you to the community.

The explanation given to me for why Grandpa so rarely visited was that it lacked the good hospitals his fragile heart needed. He was a poet and a scholar who researched the literature associated with our mourning traditions, but he didn't bring his own children home for Moharram.

I argue with Mom: I do not recall Grandpa saying that we belong to Muhammadabad. What he did say was that there were only two things Azamgarh was known for. The first was imarti, a deep-fried tightly coiled whorl of flour, soaked in sugar syrup. The second was goondagardi. Goondaism.

Goonda is an Indian-English word. This is not necessarily a professional gangster, but someone liable to attack or intimidate people. The Uttar Pradesh Control of Goondas Act (1970) describes a goonda as a habitual offender in matters of public obscenity or causing disharmony between communities (religious, linguistic, racial, caste and so on), illegal possession of arms, a gambler, a tout, a house-grabber, or someone 'reputed to be a person who is desperate and dangerous to the community'.

I was too young to ask my grandfather what it meant to belong to a place that's rich in sugarcane, poetry and goondas. By the time I began to wonder, he was gone. It was left to me to sift through words, memories and the land itself for answers.

*

I visited Muhammadabad Gohna and Karhan a few times, partly to appease Mom and partly out of curiosity.

It's true about the imarti. Row upon row of imartis line the sweet shops. Coils of pure sugar shock. In winter, you see mounds of gur (jaggery) sold by the kilo off handcarts.

There's a railway station, too short for the long trains that come through. Once, my mother failed to disembark because the compartment she was in was so far out on the railway track that the platform wasn't even visible. Peering out of the window, she assumed the train had halted in the middle of nowhere. When I heard, I bit my tongue and stopped myself from saying what I was thinking: it *is* the middle of nowhere.

It certainly isn't the sort of place where you can call an Uber. I've begun to step out nevertheless, unaccompanied by menfolk and uncaring of tradition. I neither wear a burqa nor the 'Syed' prefix, used by families to indicate descent from the Prophet Muhammad. Yet, tradition follows me wherever I go.

One day, I decided to brave a bone-rattling journey to visit a library in another village. Four modes of transport – a cycle rickshaw, an auto-rickshaw, a bus, a car – were needed to cover a distance of about thirty odd kilometres. Sixteen adults, each of them in better humour than me, were packed into a modified auto-rickshaw that was originally built to ferry four passengers. The village roads were so pitted, the only thing that prevented me from being violently jolted and tossed out of the vehicle was the fact that I was packed in so tight, mercifully between two other women, that movement was impossible.

The elderly woman on my right kept up a cheerful banter in a Bhojpuri dialect that was so far removed from Hindi, she may as well have been talking French. Finally, she asked where I came from. I caught the word *ghar*. Home.

I said, I'm from here, from Muhammadabad actually.

The elderly woman gave me a sideways stare. 'From Syedwada?'

It wasn't a question. One glance and she had me pinned to my street: Syedwada, a neighbourhood filled with Syed Muslim families, was stamped on my face, my accent, my clothes, my gestures, my obvious disconnect with the world outside home. Even without the veil, and despite my mixed blood inheritance, she could tell.

I didn't bother to deny it. I didn't ask how she could tell. I know my country enough by now to know how.

*

Rajeev Yadav is a human rights activist from the same approximate region, what used to be the undivided Azamgarh. Unlike
me, he grew up there. When I put to him the puzzle of what my
grandfather said – about imarti and goondagardi – he came back
with: 'You must be Savarn Muslim.'

Sa-varn. Upper caste. I was taken aback at first. Of course, a sort
of caste system does exist among Muslims, and Sikhs and
Christians. Still, that my family's worldview could be coloured
by caste was not a thought I'd entertained. I should have known
better. Muslims in the eastern districts have always been highly
stratified with Syeds, Shaikhs, Raqis (people who claimed to be
Iraqis who migrated a couple of centuries ago) and Mohammadan
Rajputs identifying as distinct communities. Like their Hindu
counterpart, 'Musalman castes' were also identified by profession
in pre-independence censuses: Darzis, Qasabs, Telis, Bhangis,
Dhobis, Mughals, Bhat, Kuneras, Dafalis, Kunjras, Nats.[1]

I'd heard that certain castes, who had very small landholdings of their own, served as the *lath-baaz* (stick wielders) for
bigger landlords. I turned to another Azamgarh native and
human rights activist, Naseeruddin Sanjari, to ask what was
implied by that. He pointed out that landlords in the late nineteenth and twentieth centuries had been more or less reduced
to being revenue collectors for the British government. They
maintained *pehelwans* (wrestlers) and lath-baaz to serve as
guards, or to help collect revenue from peasants. Besides, the
stick was wielded to make sure everyone treated landlords
with the respect to which they felt entitled. The landlords
were thus one step removed from the physical enactment of
aggression.

Land was the main identity. Bigger landlords had civil relationships with each other across religious lines, and were often
upper caste. The outcastes, Dalits, rarely owned land. Scholars
have noted that eastern Uttar Pradesh remained semi-feudal
well into the 1990s, with 72 per cent of workers dependent on
farming. Roger Jeffery and Jens Lerche have observed that the
lack of social development was linked to the 'uncompromising
character of its upper class and upper caste elite'.[2]

In other words, the elites refused to relinquish control over land, refused to share power in ways that would fulfil the promise of democracy. This caused sharp imbalances between east and west within the same state. A 2005 study by the state's planning department used twenty-nine development indicators and found that of the twenty most developed districts, fifteen were in the west, and of the least developed twenty districts, seventeen were in the east.[3] Among the least developed districts were Azamgarh and Mau.

South of the Ghagra river, criss-crossed by a dozen smaller rivers with names that conjure distinct personalities, the land has been fertile for longer than anyone remembers. This is part of a civilisation that offers us the pithy phrase '*jar, joru, jameen*' or '*zar, zan, zameen*' – 'gold, woman, land' – the three things men fight over. Of these, land is the hardest to guard since it cannot be locked away. To guard the land, one needs other men, or guns. My mother told me of her surprise when she learnt that a gentle-mannered cousin was riding about his farm in Karhan with a gun. He explained, it was unavoidable. You had land, you guarded it. There was very little land left anyway. Grandpa had none. He used to have an old gun, though none of us ever saw it. His temperament can be judged by the story Mom tells about how he behaved when a snake entered the house. He pulled on a pair of thick leather shoes and called the cops.

My grandparents had quit the land. They didn't live off farming. Very few could. The district gazetteer of 1922 – in the midst of my grandfather's early childhood years – noted that, despite its fertility and suitable climate, Azamgarh barely produced enough food to feed itself. But did that make people violent?

Not especially. In 1922, the gazetteer also noted that 'on the whole, crime is light', going up only in times of famine. Offences against public tranquillity and trespass were common problems, though; landowners were 'particularly tenacious of their rights and quick to resent any supposed or real encroachment'.

What happened to this fabled tenacity in our family? How did my grandfather let go so easily of his share of land?

I look for answers in his memoir, *Gubār-e-Karvān* (Dust left behind by a caravan), where he describes a *jāgīrdārāna māhaul*, the landlords' environment. Up until the early twentieth century, landlords' homes were like miniature fortresses, with gardens, stores, kitchens, *kuchehri* (entertainment hall), *imāmbārās*, cellars, stables, offices, double-storeyed living quarters. He also confirmed the tradition of *begār*. People cleaned, managed animals, cooked, worked hand-held fans, but what they were paid was given as reward for good service, not a wage they could demand as their right.

When he was 13, his father died and his link to the land started to weaken. A great-uncle took him away to Mahmudabad, a princely estate near Lucknow, for a modern education. Exciting cultural conversations were unfolding in campuses and newspaper offices at the time. Grandpa got entangled in student politics and fell in with the progressive writers' movement. He began to write poems against imperialism, oppression and blind traditionalism. In the 1940s, revolution was not an empty idea. Many students were socialists and freedom fighters. Grandpa, too, was arrested and put in jail for a few months.

Later, he did return to practise law in Azamgarh and the neighbouring Ghazipur court. There was, however, little to keep him there. Azamgarh birthed many writers but few of them actually lived there. Grandpa, too, returned to Lucknow and its vibrant world of letters, and, from 1946 onwards, worked for the Indian government in various media and cultural roles. Transfers meant uprooting himself and his family every few years, but this didn't seem to bother him. Perhaps he just liked living in cities. Perhaps he only cared about finding literary friends and doing the work he felt was his own to do.

There was no mention of brute violence in his memoir, though. What could have triggered his careless jibe about goondagardi?

*

Rajeev Yadav reminded me that the ruin of Azamgarh's reputation can be traced to 1857. The rebels who first rode into Delhi, having mutinied against the British East India Company, were mainly Purbia: soldiers from the eastern districts who caused mayhem in Delhi. Plunder by soldiers was not new, of course, but 1857 was an enormously disruptive event and this absolute breakdown of order became linked with Purbias.

Azamgarh was a crucial site during the uprising. It was here that an *Ishtehār* (proclamation) was issued, perhaps by one of the grandsons of the last Mughal emperor. It sought to overthrow the English, who 'had ruined each class of citizen – zamindaar, merchant, civil servants, soldiers, artisans and even the clergy', but more interesting, it also served as a kind of pre-democratic manifesto, with promises that the restored Badshahi (royal) government would resolve the problems of each class.[4]

The aftermath was brutal. Thousands were executed, more exiled. It became harder for Purbias to find employment as soldiers. Many were forced into indentured labour in foreign colonies. There was a difference too in the way the British treated landlords and nobles of the eastern, central and western districts. The west gained from agricultural improvements like canals, less fragmented landholdings, less harsh taxes imposed on the actual tillers of the land. Meanwhile, the eastern landlords incurred mounting debts and allowed sub-tenanting; there was no significant investment by the government.

After India gained independence, the feudal system continued in all but name. Landowners no longer faced the same kind of oppressive revenues demanded by the British government, but they continued to extract wage-less labour. Hindi writer Shiv Prasad Singh set his landmark 1967 novel *Alag Alag Vaitarni* in a village in eastern Uttar Pradesh, describing complex caste equations where those who are higher up the ladder depend heavily on lower-caste labour, but behave as if they were doing the latter a favour. A character of the Chamar caste is beaten for refusing to work in the fields without a wage in the middle of a drought. Weeping, he contrasts his situation with that of a group of nomadic Chamars who do the same work, but with a measure of dignity: in refusing to put down roots, they can refuse to beg the upper castes for a bit of land to till or to build their huts. To him, they appear free as birds, and he reflects that the most fragile hut can turn into a shackle for people who do not own land.

After independence, there were some efforts at land distribution. There was a ceiling on how much land an individual could hold. Many landlords legally transferred lands to relatives or employees, but did not relinquish control. This probably required that a degree of fear be instilled in the hearts of those who were owners on paper, but dared not act as if they were.

The feudal lords of yore were also establishing new founts of power and wealth. They became politicians, contractors, real estate dealers. Sticks were eventually replaced with guns.

*

In the twenty-first century, vast swathes of north India have developed a reputation for goondaism. There are islands of exception: Lucknow especially had a reputation for refinement and extreme politesse, and, being the state capital, was easier monitored. But Uttar Pradesh has been described as a pit-stop to hell, and even as a failed state.[5]

Part of me rears up in defence. I want to say, this is unfair stereotyping. But there's no getting away from the fact that the state tops the crime charts. According to the National Crime Records Bureau, some 3.06 million crimes were recorded under the Indian Penal Code in 2017, of which Uttar Pradesh accounted for the highest number: 310,084.[6]

I want to dodge, and point to more obfuscating data: Kerala is one of the least populated, best-educated states, but it has the highest crime rate in the country. Even Maharashtra and Rajasthan have higher crime rates than Uttar Pradesh. Trouble is, I know the crime rate is based on reportage, even of minor assaults and skirmishes, and can be indicative of public faith in the system or an unwillingness to be cowed down by goons. As a percentage of its population, Uttar Pradesh reports a crime rate only marginally higher than the tiny islands of Andaman and Nicobar, which are home to primitive tribes and where only 638 crimes have been reported. It just doesn't add up. Chances are, someone has been fudging data.[7] It is also likely that people are too scared to report crime, and things are probably worse than they look on paper.

One way to look at aggression is to look at guns. The risk of gang violence and intimidation is higher with more guns floating around. The legal firearm possession rate in 2016 was highest in Uttar Pradesh;[8] it also records the highest number of violations of the Arms Act of 1959. There's no accounting for the extent of illegal weapons, but there is a well-documented cottage industry in basic rifles and hand-held guns called *desi katta* or *tamancha*. Until a few years ago, it was possible to get one made for anything between 1,200 and 5,000 rupees (USD 17 and 70).

Guns have been manufactured by rural ironsmiths for centuries.[9] The trade was above board and the clientele was mainly farmers or regional armies.[10] However, since firearms have required licences, the trade has slipped into the grey market. A small, localised industry has grown into a cross-country trade. Some of the demand is driven by gangsters, but manufacturers have also suggested that police officials also acquire *desi kattas*, to plant on people they want to arrest.[11] Police officials are not known for being sticklers for rules. This state also reports the highest number of custodial deaths and suspected 'fake encounters',[12] wherein police personnel kill people in cold blood after abducting and assaulting them. Some of those killed are petty thieves and goons; some are merely suspected of crime; most are poor.

\*

It wasn't until I started asking around that I heard a similar stereotype about *western* Uttar Pradesh, that it was famous for two things: the sweetness of its cane juice, and its gang wars.[13]

Violence is certainly not limited to Azamgarh. In the national capital, Delhi, you might see notices at eateries

advising patrons that firearms are not permitted. I have seen
notices painted in buses in the neighbouring state, Madhya
Pradesh, asking passengers not to carry *loaded* guns. If such
warnings are any indication, then people do carry guns when
they're out for pizza or checking out the price of corn. What
may be specific to the eastern districts is an intersection of
feudal habits, joblessness and politicians working in tandem
with business contractors.

There was a theory afoot in the 1970s and 1980s that economic
development would help combat goondaism. The government's
policies had the opposite effect. Funds poured in by way of state-
funded road construction and railway projects. Those who profited from aggression quickly got organised. Whoever had more
weapons and money began to grab more contracts, and eventually made inroads into politics. The highway to the heart of
power began to be laid with blood and bullets.

Still. It bothered me that Azamgarh had the worse reputation
when there's Gorakhpur right next door. Now *that's* a district
where local gangsters have been described as 'a herd of
Capones'.[14] From Gorakhpur emerged Hari Shankar Tiwari, the
first alleged gangster to win an election whilst lodged in prison.
He won six elections straight, supported by various political
parties, and was acquitted of all charges eventually.[15] He and
his arch rival Virendra Pratap Shahi, also from Gorakhpur,
started out in the 1970s. Reports suggest that their early adven-
tures were classic goondagardi: taking over land that belonged to
someone else, refusing to pay for fuel at petrol pumps, abusing
anyone who dared to look them straight in the eye. By the 1980s,
both groups – Brahmin and Thakur – were running a sort of
parallel administration. People were going to them rather than
to the courts to resolve land disputes or other conflicts.[16] From
there to becoming actual administrators was one short step.

In the 1980s, elections were sometimes captured through
intimidating voters and taking over booths. Once people saw
that the judiciary and government appeared powerless to prevent such capture, they decided to transfer their mandate to
whoever was able to get things done.

Raghuraj Singh, better known as Raja Bhaiyya (literally 'king brother'), comes from minor royalty and was once described as the 'Gunda (goon) of Kunda' by a former chief minister, who later bestowed a ministerial berth upon the same man he had derided.[17] In western Uttar Pradesh, there was Mangu Tyagi, who, as one cop put it, has been charged under 'almost every section of the Indian Penal Code' including murder, abduction, extortion, possession of illegal arms, arson and so on.[18] That didn't interfere with his nomination by a mainstream political party.

Dhananjay Singh, who has been described as 'mafia-turned-politician', didn't even need political parties.[19] He won as an independent candidate in 2002.

One of the most powerful men in the Azamgarh-Mau region is Mukhtar Ansari, who won Mau four times.[20] Reports have described him as a sort of 'Robinhood boss', the man you went to if you needed money for your daughter's wedding or a job for your son, or to keep the local textile industry up and running. He has been in jail too, accused of various crimes including murder and goondaism.

Such men are often described as *bahubali* (strongman), and their power can be gauged from the spectacular fashion in which they clash. When a politician known to have links with a gangster was killed while in transit, it was estimated that at least 400 bullets had been fired from AK-47 rifles.

The police in India don't have easy access to automatic weapons. Nearly half the police force has been using weaponry declared outdated twenty years ago.[21] In 2017, it emerged that 267 police stations didn't even have telephones and 273 stations had no transportation vehicle. Over 45 per cent of the police stations minus telephones were in Uttar Pradesh.

A monk from the order of Nath Jogis became chief minister of the state in 2017. Yogi Adityanath alias Ajay Singh Bisht was once quoted as saying, 'I find western UP unsafe. We do not face a threat in eastern UP because there we use the language that people understand and set them straight.'[22] He too had three charges of rioting against him, one attempt to murder, one charge of endangering others' lives, two cases of trespassing on burial places, one charge related to criminal intimidation.[23] After he assumed office, all charges were dismissed.

Meanwhile, the chainmail linking guns, businessmen and the formal political system has got stronger with each election cycle. At the time of writing, 106 of the 521 members of Parliament have been booked for crimes such as murder, inciting communal disharmony, kidnapping and rape. Here too, Uttar Pradesh leads.

*

It wasn't always like this. There was a time Azamgarh was a socialist stronghold. Local leaders raised slogans like: *Ye azaadi jhooti hai; desh ki janta bhooki hai.* Our freedom is a lie; the people are still hungry.

In the 1980s, however, the political culture changed dramatically, and the reputation for poetry and textiles was replaced by a reputation for lawless men who had little to lose. Mumbai's mafia was partly to blame. The gangs were hiring freelance shooters, paying as little as INR 5,000–10,000 (USD 70–140) for a hit job.[24] These killings served as warnings through which millions could be extorted from potential victims.[25] The young men who killed for such paltry sums often had no criminal records and, after the hit, melted back into the landscape from where they had come. Some of them, however, were traced to Azamgarh and this small town acquired a reputation for danger rather than Mumbai, which was home to an underworld described as a 'well-oiled machine' with an annual turnover several times the municipal budget.[26]

Goons and gangs, however, were not as damaging as the third round of stereotyping. This time it was linked to *terror* – a word deployed with terrifying precision, for terrifying ends.

Azamgarh has had few moments of communal tension. However, a narrative has been drummed up that seeks to isolate and demonise Muslims ever since a mob led by Hindutva organisations demolished the Babri Masjid in 1992, followed by riots and bomb attacks. In subsequent years, the Students' Islamic Movement of India was banned under anti-terror laws and among its office bearers were men who had origins in Azamgarh.

The narrative around Azamgarh grew wings in 2008. After a series of bomb blasts in Delhi, the police claimed that suspects were hiding in a place called Batla House. Police killed two young men, both from Azamgarh, arrested a third, and claimed that two others escaped.

Concerted efforts have since been made to paint the whole district with the brush of terror. These are really efforts to reconfigure a political constituency that has traditionally voted centre or left.

Yogi Adityanath has considerable influence in seven eastern UP districts but less so in Azamgarh and Mau. His influence is exercised through organisations like Hindu Yuva Vahani, Hindu Jagran Manch and several others. Some of their members' interventions led, in part, to the Mau riots of 2005.

It started, as it usually does, with contested space: land, right of way, cultural assertation. A Hindu festival was coinciding with Ramzan. A citizens' investigation later found that the 2005 riot could have been prevented, were it not for aggressive posturing by groups like the Hindu Yuva Vahani. Citizens who attempted to keep the peace were accused of cowardice.[27]

The legislator at the time was Mukhtar Ansari. He has been arrested on various counts over the years, but during the Mau riot he was out and trying to calm people down. However, when a video surfaced, television channels broadcast it with the sound muted. Nobody could tell that Ansari was trying to stop the riot: all they saw was a Muslim representative out with his men. Newspapers went further. The *Times of India* carried a front-page headline saying, 'Feeling of insecurity grips Hindus in Mau', giving the impression that Hindus were being targeted when in fact Muslims were the terrified minority.

One of the writers of the citizens' report, V. N. Rai, is a retired cop and the author of an analysis of communal riots in India. He found great anti-Muslim bias within the police force and a gross under-representation of Muslims in the police and the armed constabulary.[28] This bias has been reconfirmed in recent surveys, which show that many police officers believe Muslims and Dalits are more prone to committing crimes.[29]

Over the last two decades, dozens of young Muslim men have been picked up without much evidence and tortured for years while in custody. Rajeev Yadav and his colleagues have set up an organisation called Rihai Manch that works specifically on finding legal redress for such youths.

Instead of addressing institutional bias, the home minister of India[30] as well as the chief minister of the state continue to make statements linking Azamgarh with terrorism.[31] This serves the dual purpose of isolating and frightening Muslims while preventing the Hindu majority from taking pride in their regional identity, thus shattering old bonds of regional affiliation and class solidarity.

*

The phrase 'native place' has great currency in India. People use it as an English substitute for Hindi words like *mulk* and *vatan*, which refer to both country and home. Migrant workers sometimes disappear from city jobs for weeks, and enquiries reveal that they have gone to their mulk. It is where families and farmlands are, or where they trace their roots, as we do in eastern Uttar Pradesh.

On my first visit here, I found the soothing flatness of the horizon reach into some part of me that wants to be captured, the way trees capture earth. I remember looking at the remnants of a crumbling wall made of flat *lakhori* bricks, trees growing out of the walls of my great-grandmother's kitchen, and thinking, is this my vatan?

I keep an eye open for goondaism: raised voices, fisticuffs, a revolver or rifle, glowering eyes. What I find instead is patience and forbearance, and a poverty so keen that sixteen people routinely squish into a vehicle meant for four. Passengers quibble over a single rupee worth of carriage fare. One Indian rupee can no longer buy anything, not even the sugary imarti. But ten such trips where one rupee is saved after humiliating bargains could add up to one sweet for a child waiting at home. I notice how thin every-one is.

I watch poorly made videos on YouTube about how to make jaggery: women stripping cane, mud stove, a vat, the drape and fall of cheap sarees, shawls in winter. These are not my mem-ories. My mother would never drape a saree in that style, nor does she know her way around a wood-fired stove. Why does it all look familiar?

I go looking for artists and find a national Sangeet Natak award-winning[32] theatre director and a troupe called Sutradhar that performs in a cinema hall with perforated walls that stopped screening movies long ago. The group per-forms and people are encouraged to pay 5 rupees, because that's what it costs to rent a chair for the evening. On good days, I'm told, busloads of people travel hours to watch a performance.

In my head, I tell my grandfather: *It's not a cultural desert.*

In my head, I see him smile at my bristling defence as if he were glad, but also sceptical: *Are you moving here, then?*

No. This might have been our vatan, his and mine, but it's not our *zameen*. The word *zameen* also has dual connotations. It means land, but also a certain psychological environment. It is soil, mood, air, culture, space. It can be prepared, created, levelled, ruined. It is where you blossom and fructify. You make *it* as much as you need it to make yourself.

Grandpa didn't want to spell it out, but he was probably wary of the vigilance, the tenacity that land requires. He didn't hold onto his father's land and he never bought any himself. His zameen was language and literature, and there he remained comfortably rooted all his life. And how different am I?

Lying on a hard floor in Mom's morsel-sized room, in the middle of yet another power cut, I watch the ancestral sky turn a deep Prussian blue, and I wonder if I am making a mistake, looking for roots that I can't quite put down.

Even so, I have begun to tell people that my roots are in district Mau-formerly-in-Azamgarh. Its reputation stopped bothering me once I woke up to the fractured nature of law enforcement and the limitations of a judicial process that's heavily dependent on a biased, unrepresentative and under-equipped police force.

One of the men who win elections, in or out of jail, had famously declared that even God can't control crime in this state.[33] Sometimes I think, maybe God has a good reason for not intervening. What does it mean: law, crime, goondaism? Whose crimes are annulled, whose crimes magnified? If a man can be tempted to board a train from his village to Mumbai to kill a stranger for 5,000 rupees, one has to ask: who is being made to feel that human life is cheap?

Every day, we see reports of laws being used against those who go looking for justice, and allegations of police failing to collect or present evidence in court, or cultivating false testimony, or killing or raping people in custody. Some are crimes so brutal, the only thing that makes them worse is the knowledge that they were perpetrated by men in uniform, and that the individual was not stopped by the conscience of the collective. There is very little standing between the unarmed citizen and the abyss.

Goondagardi is not a label that can be tacked onto any specific geography. I now see goondaism and policing, law and outlaw, not as separate categories but as behaviours. In places where people are aware that right and wrong is different from legal and illegal, and where the simplest way of getting on the right side of the law is to become a lawmaker yourself, words like *lawlessness* have little meaning. If you emerge unscathed from such places, if you escape feudalism, caste, bigotry, corruption, hunger, and someone else's rage, be grateful. *There, but for the grace of God . . .*

Still, you have to recognise the crucible, and if you can put anything good into it, do so. Maybe that's what Grandpa meant by, never forget your roots?

Nowadays when people mention the goondaism in my native place, I react like a cow chewing cud. I resist expostulation and say, yeah, the imarti is famous too.

India is home to 122 distinct languages of which Hindi can claim the greatest number of speakers.

# 3 LISTENING TO MOTHER

Maya Angelou has said that 'the ache for home lives in all of us. The safe place where we can go as we are and not be questioned.'[1]

This safe place – does it exist? I don't know. What I do know is that the illusion must exist. For a person to give her loyalty to the land, to trust those who create and enforce laws, safety is a prerequisite. One essential aspect to this illusion is familiarity: systems functioning as we expect them to, people talking in tongues we understand.

When a friend posted on Facebook that Hindi was his mother while Urdu was his beloved, I understood at once what he meant. A mother tongue, simultaneously soothing and challenging with its elastic grace, is the topsoil of attachment. There are few things as affirming as being able to tap into cultural nuance through words: literature of course, but also dialect, inflection of tone, idiom, being able to interpret silences.

Conversely, there are few things as disorienting as being in a place where you lack the language. Anxiety had crept up on me the first few of times I was in south India where street signs were in Malayalam, Tamil, Kannada: all unfamiliar scripts.

The anxiety was difficult to acknowledge since I was not in a foreign country. It was startling, too, for I had not yet started thinking of language as a chariot of power, though I myself inhabited two of the most powerful languages in the country.

Looking back, it is amazing that I should have been so clueless. Mine was the generation that grew up watching advertisements for the Rapidex English Speaking Course. It was ubiquitous: businesses promising English fluency in a matter of weeks. This was intended as a supplement to regular schooling. Middle-class Indians scrambled to use every bit of influence they possessed to get their wards admitted to 'convents', schools established by English or French missionaries. Affluent parents who resented Christian cultural influences nevertheless strove for admission, and it became lucrative to append 'St' (saint) to any private school's name.

The college I attended was church-run and some of the nuns did not hide their despair at how many girls enrolled to improve their marital prospects. Matrimonial advertisements sometimes included 'convented' among the list of feminine virtues such as 'homely' and 'beautiful'. The word signalled a measure of discipline, a decent education and, of course, English.

Hindi scholar Francesca Orsini observed in a lecture on multilingual education that many Indians talked of their own language as a handicap. The most sought-after schools were those that could help kids overcome this handicap. Some insisted that students speak exclusively in English and petty fines were imposed to ensure obedience. School libraries stocked mainly English books.

Even in multilingual cities like Mumbai, which had aggressive movements for Marathi and against English and Hindi, the suburbs were plastered with advertisements offering 'English' through images of youths dressed in western suits, a laptop or file in their hands. Language was key to jobs.

It was assumed that most Indians would also inhabit a 'home' language, but this was not necessarily true. My own parents had to make a conscious decision not to speak English all the time. Mom says she didn't want us growing up not knowing the 'ka-ki of Hindi', that is, failing to use the correct gendered pronoun. Hindi was best picked up in infancy. And so, Hindi with some inflections of Urdu, or Hindustani as it was called, became my mother tongue. However, since my parents were bilingual, as were my aunts and uncles, English became an equal mother tongue, one that was nourished better through an unstinting supply of literature.

As a child, I failed to understand my classmates' struggles with grammar workbooks. I never had to reach for answers; the knowledge was fused with my bones. It was only after I moved to Mumbai that I confronted my first linguistic hurdle: I did not speak Marathi. Still, I didn't feel quite shut out since the Marathi script is nearly identical to Hindi. I also had a year of Gujarati in school and could read simple sentences. In this way, I always had partial access to the city.

However, in Mumbai, I could no longer take Hindi for granted and that's when I started to pay heed. I would overhear phone conversations and pick out an Avadhi or Purbia accent, and I discovered that listening brought quiet pleasure, like cracking one's knuckles or walking in the sand. The accent broke through my natural reserve. I found myself initiating conversations with strangers, even mock-arguing with vendors just for the pleasure of listening to them talk. There were clues to religion, class, caste and education embedded in accent, but once we got talking, we momentarily transcended our differences. For a little while, we stood on level ground.

Still, it wasn't until I started travelling in rural India that I realised how at home I was in my own language, how out of place in another, and what was at stake.

*

There are twenty-two scheduled languages in India; that is, languages listed in the eighth schedule of the constitution. In addition to these, the government acknowledges 19,500 languages and dialects.[2] Of these, 122 are recognised as distinct languages.[3] An independent study, the People's Linguistic Survey of India edited by Ganesh Devy, suggests that 780 languages and 68 scripts are currently in use.

The 2011 census shows that 44 per cent of India identifies as Hindi speaking, but only about 21 per cent, or 257 million Indians, call it a mother tongue.[4] There are 49 languages embedded within the broad category of 'Hindi'. Ganesh Devy suggests there are at least 65 languages classified as 'variants', although these are quite different. Someone like me, for instance, has very poor access to Bhojpuri as it is spoken in rural Azamgarh. I cannot sustain the simplest conversations.

In Uttar Pradesh, a state described as the 'Hindi heartland', the imposition of Hindi as a formal language has not been without pain. Bhojpuri and Braj did not wither away and fall off children's tongues like so much deadweight. They've often had to be whipped out of children, with teachers shaming or punishing students for talking like illiterates.[5]

The link between language recognition, language alienation and democratic values is profound. When I started reporting from villages in the 'Hindi belt' (states in north, central and western India where Hindi is the official language), I often needed the help of someone who has been in the formal school system long enough to interpret. This someone had to be willing to interpret, had to have a sufficient Hindi vocabulary to prevent misunderstandings, and also had to have the trust of others in the community. It was a very tall order. Yet this was the order of things, not only for visitors like me but for the state executive and administration. States like Rajasthan have been using Hindi as the sole official language although a significant chunk of their population does not consider it a mother tongue. What this translates into is the state talking to people who cannot talk back.

It is bewildering, even scary, to get a notice from the government or the municipality and not be able to fully comprehend it. These are matters of life and death – being asked for proof of citizenship, procurement of land, tax arrears, warnings to not venture into the forest or into the sea, information about free healthcare, supplementary diets, court summonses. Whoever controls language, controls everything.

Naturally, Hindi speakers have a lot vested in making it *the* language of India, though they have met with vociferous opposition. Soon after independence, a representative did not hesitate to say that, if Hindi were to be the sole official language, the Indian union would have to do without the south. A compromise was reached and the removal of English as an official language was postponed until 1965. It was assumed that all of India would warm to Hindi and reject English as a colonial vestige. This did not happen, despite 'hectic mobilisations' as described in *Hindi Nationalism*.[6] An aggressive '*Angrezi hatao*' ('Remove English') campaign was matched by anti-Hindi protests. In Madras, there was rioting and arson, and dozens of people were killed by paramilitary forces before the central government backed down.

Other states also resisted the threat of sociopolitical dominance. Pushback came in the form of mandatory signage in regional languages like Marathi, Bengali and Kannada, and a refusal to use Hindi in state communication. In 2017, a conference attempted to unite non-Hindi states to fight 'Hindi chauvinism'[7] and, in 2018, a Bengali advocacy group advocated against 'Hindi imperialism'.[8]

In other states, Hindi prevailed by denying 'language' status to potential challengers. In 1949, an Adivasi representative had asked that Mundari, Gondi and Oraon languages be included in the eighth schedule; they boasted over 4 million, 3 million and 1 million speakers respectively.[9] The demand was turned down on the grounds that these languages lacked a written script. There were even attempts to deny Punjabi by calling it a dialect of Hindi, although it was written in three distinct scripts.

Language cannot fail to be a political tool in a federal system of governance and where states are organised along linguistic lines. Bhojpuri, for instance, is a mother tongue for 33 million 'Hindi' speakers, and an additional 6 million in the international diaspora.[10] This is nearly twice the population of the Netherlands and half that of France. Its speakers demand full language status. Successive governments acknowledged the legitimacy of the demand but were slow to act on it because Bhojpuri is linked to a politically coherent region. There has been a long-standing demand for a trifurcation of Uttar Pradesh, by separating the east, west and central districts. If Bhojpuri is elevated to a language equal in status to Punjabi, the demand for a separate state will gather steam.

Adivasi activists have also begun to develop written scripts and compile dictionaries to preserve languages, and scripts may give political self-expression a leg up. The demand for Gondwana, a territorial homeland for Gond tribespeople in central India, emerged during the 1940s, but was denied. To this day, many Gonds don't use languages like Hindi or Marathi. Activists say it is rare to find journalists, government officials, even teachers who can speak Gondi. The language barrier leads to misunderstandings with the government, and primary education remains an uphill task.[11]

'Officiating' languages complicate the texture of citizenship. In 2000, a new state called Chhattisgarh was finally carved out of central India, but it continued to use Hindi as the state language, even though Chhattisgarhi is a distinct language spoken by over 16 million people. The state has a significant ST population, over 30 per cent, and Hindi is not a mother tongue for any of the tribes. Twenty years have passed. The state website offers information mainly in Hindi, partially in English. There are no toggle buttons for Chhattisgarhi or Gondi.

The same year, parts of Uttar Pradesh were also carved out into a new state, Uttarakhand, which also continues to use Hindi on the grounds that it is understood widely. However, tribes that live in the Himalayan foothills struggle. Travelling in the region, I found that while they may understand what I'm saying, many people in rural hamlets are barely on nodding terms with Hindi. They pick it up in school but lose much of the vocabulary once they retreat into a life of farming, shepherding or labour. This is especially true for women. Yet, when Uttarakhand adopted a second official language, Sanskrit was chosen over and above the claims of languages like Garhwali or Kumaoni, spoken by millions of people in the state.[12]

Sanskrit is claimed as a mother tongue by just 24,821 Indians and is officially classified as 'N', where N stands for negligible.[13]

*

In *Hindi Nationalism*, Alok Rai describes language as an intimate possession: something that one possesses in the same measure that one is possessed by, and which is 'tied up with the foundations of one's being'.[14]

Hindustani, a colloquial Hindi which was nearer Urdu, was indeed my possession. The Sanskrit-infused version of Hindi taught in school was a burden I bore reluctantly. It was as if the syllabus had been designed to test how far the envelope of comprehension could be pushed. The Hindi of movies, songs, friends, of contemporary poetry and fiction, was like a cosy room with a rug on the floor. Official Hindi was like sitting on a stone floor on cold winter nights.

The problem, as Rai puts it, is that Hindi has always been 'in a state of war'.[15] Until the mid nineteenth century, the words *Hindi* and *Urdu* were used interchangeably, so slender was the difference. Urdu drew upon Braj, Sanksrit, Persian, dozens of 'tongues' that developed concurrently. It also moved up in the world – from a commoner's language, it became a literary language flourishing in the eighteenth and nineteenth centuries. In written form, it used Nastaliq, drawing on Persian, which was a court language in Delhi. Those who wanted jobs in administration, even at the lower clerical orders, had to learn the script.

Rai has compared the British decision to extirpate all signs and symbols of 'the old India' to the Nazi treatment of symbols of Jewish influence in Europe. 'The physical locations, the institutions and the relationships, the fabric that sustained and sheltered that world were ripped to shreds.'[16] Key to that fabric was a common language. There had been demands from a section of Hindus who sought state jobs via the Nāgri script, and the government eventually recognised 'Hindi' as a language separate from Urdu. The two were soon locked in 'a bitter complementarity, each matching the extravagant excesses of the other'. Sanskrit was poured into the vessel of Hindi while Urdu-wallas injected more Persian.

In 1943, journalist Makhanlal Chaturvedi warned that forcing Sanskrit into Hindi not only destroyed its natural fluency, it also lent ideological support to the demand for a separate homeland for Muslims.[17] This was more or less how things played out. With a split tongue, the idea of two people, two nations became an easier sell.

The making of a new Hindi is what Rai calls 'a narrative of intimate destabilisation and dispossession'.[18] It was a dispossession that severed me from my own cultural moorings. My grandfather was an Urdu writer. He could speak Bhojpuri since he was raised in a village, and was formally tutored in English, Urdu, Persian, Arabic. When he joined the freedom struggle and was jailed, he used the time to learn to read and write the Nāgri script. He even began to use some Sanskrit-inflected Hindi words in his poetry. Many of his generation learnt both scripts not just for professional reasons but also to improve cultural understanding and solidarity. However, the Partition of India undid all such efforts.

When it was created, Pakistan chose Urdu as a national language though none of its provinces had a majority of Urdu speakers. It was a refugee language. Meanwhile, in its homeland, Urdu met with greater distrust as the intimate possession of Pakistan. By the 1960s, Indian poet-film lyricist Sahir Ludhianvi complained – in metre and rhyme – that Urdu, while being nominally celebrated, was being treated as the enemy language. In 1967, a communal riot was instigated when the state of Bihar chose Urdu as its second official language, even though it was indeed the second most widely understood language. Anti-Urdu pamphlets were distributed at the time, describing the move as a challenge to the manhood of a new generation.[19]

My mother was not taught Urdu in school. She could read and write it, but only ever used Urdu to write letters to my grandmother, who couldn't read anything else. When I was in school, English and Hindi medium schools taught English and Hindi as two major languages. A third language was mandated but most schools chose Sanskrit. Many students, unable to appreciate a language far removed from both experience and aspiration, made up whiny rhymes. A popular one referenced the grammatical grid that we had to mug up:

> *Lata, Latey, Lataani*
> *Humko Sanskrit nahin aani*
> *Aani bhi to bhool jaani*
> *Master-ji se maar khaani*

> Lata, Latey, Lataani
> We will never learn Sanskrit
> If we learn, we will forget
> The schoolmaster will beat us

Marwari, Mewari, Bheeli, Bhojpuri, Avadhi, Braj – any of these would have been valuable for students who were trying to inhabit a culturally complex state like Rajasthan. However, the idea would not be entertained because these were not considered 'languages' at all. Urdu would have been useful because it would teach a new script, and would help heal the wounds of Partition. But schools would not teach it.

Sanskrit, on the other hand, saw concerted attempts at revival. Several universities have Sanskrit departments and there are universities devoted exclusively to it. Regardless of the lack of demand from students, the government has introduced a new law seeking to set up Sanskrit Central Universities. One MP has gone to the extent of declaring that speaking Sanskrit helps control diabetes and cholesterol.[20]

*

Language politics is knotted into origin politics. Origin myths decide who has first claim on bread and stone, cotton and salt. The question of who is from where, translates as who can dispossess whom.

Ancient rulers often claimed descent from the sun or the moon, or claimed a divine right to rule since divinity did not need to respect any geographic claims. Contemporary rulers, while they are not averse to drawing legitimacy from religion, fix their 'origin' claim in land – nations, provinces, cities – and language.

In India, the question of the origin of Vedic-Sanskritic 'Aryans' is fraught with drama. I used to wonder why it mattered that ancient Aryans were proved to be immigrants: it was so far back in time that borders had little meaning. However, the Hindutva sense of belonging in India is contingent on being able to reject non-Aryan, non-Sanskrit values as non-Indian. Adherents to the religious-political ideology broadly described as 'Hindutva' point to the 'foreign' origins of Islam and Christianity, and use that to justify the denial of the cultural rights of Muslims and Christians.

They do not deny that forest- or cave-dwelling tribes are indigenous people or 'Adivasi', but the tribes can be persuaded to give up distinct cultural memories and adopt Vedic values. Social scientist M. N. Srinivas first used the word *Sanskritisation* with reference to scheduled castes and tribes adopting upper-caste cultural practices.[21] This could mean turning vegetarian, praying to new deities, adopting Brahmanical customs like dowry, virgin brides and abstinent widows. The word *Sanskritisation* was used because these changes derive from prescriptive Sanskrit texts.

However, to accept that the Aryans were central Asian animal herders who came to the subcontinent at any point in history would mean that the Sanskritic claim is not much stronger than Turkic, Mongol or Persian claims: all are migrants, give or take a couple of millennia. A lot of energy has therefore been poured into establishing that the Rig Veda, the earliest of the liturgical Sanskrit texts, was composed within the borders of contemporary India.

The Rig Veda refers to the river Saraswati, the existence and location of which have been contested.[22] Legend has it that three rivers – Ganga, Yamuna and Saraswati – met at Prayag, a point of confluence in eastern Uttar Pradesh. The Saraswati, however, has not been seen for centuries. Scholars suggest that it was possibly confused with the Harahvaiti[23] or Haraxwati, which flowed in contemporary Afghanistan.[24]

Attempts at positioning the Saraswati within India have gone quite far. A small underground aquifer was declared as evidence of a found 'river'.[25] Public money has been pumped into engineering a water body that can be seen to flow, so that it may be described as a river, however diminished.

Being able to claim that Sanskrit originated within the borders of India is important because Sanskrit is a liturgical language.[26] It is also the language that codified the varna or caste system, with its hierarchies and rules about access to knowledge and property.[27]

Laws codified in the ancient Sanskrit texts prescribe not only unequal rights but also unequal punishments. The Dharmasutra of Gautama prescribes that molten tin or lac be poured into the ears of a Shudra found attempting to listen to a Vedic recitation, and if discovered trying to recite the Vedas, to have his tongue cut off, and if he were to memorise the Vedas, to have his body 'split asunder'.[28] In another text, the Manusmriti, there are clear instructions about Brahmins being treated as social-spiritual-intellectual superiors. Shudras, the fourth and lowest caste, were not meant to own property.

Dalits (the word can be translated as 'oppressed people') are also called scheduled castes, that is, they are mentioned in the constitution as being historically disadvantaged and therefore eligible for reserved seats in education and electoral constituencies. The Manusmriti states that there are only four castes, but mentions outcastes and *Chandals*. Since no social contact was permitted, it was not envisaged that any learning was possible for Dalits, even by accident.

What was written into law 2,000 years ago continues to be reflected in patterns of asset ownership. The top 10 per cent income bracket within upper-caste groups control 60 per cent of the nation's wealth.[29] Besides, a survey conducted by India's National Council of Applied Economic Research in association with the University of Maryland found that 27 per cent of Indians admitted to participating in some form of 'untouchability' such as refusing Dalits entry to their kitchen or not allowing them to use the same kitchen utensils. Reported crime against Dalits increased 44 per cent between 2010 and 2014, and fresh reports of violence emerge daily from all parts of the country.[30]

Gujarati writer and activist Dalpat Chauhan has a short story called 'Home' where a character who lives on the 'untouchable' street dreams of a brick house. He daren't build one, even though he has money. He must approach the village council and beg permission, to which the upper-caste response is, 'If they start living in brick houses, where will we live? In a house made of gold?'

The Dalit protagonist is thrown into a panic when he is given permission, after all, with the stipulation that the ceiling be so low, one can touch it by raising one's hand, no windows face the street, no niches or cupboards. He must hire a cart belonging to one of the upper castes and even give up his pet goat as an offering. The day the house is ready, before the family can move in, it is set on fire.

Ideas have a higher chance of survival if the language in which they are embodied survives. The overwhelming emphasis on Sanskrit rather than on other ancient languages like Pali, associated with Buddhist texts, is possibly an indication of which ideas are deemed worthy of perpetuation, and who benefits.

*

One of the most telling instances of how discrimination works in the public space is the food culture in India. It is one of the few places in the world where eating meat is described as a negative or 'non', as in *I am non-vegetarian.*

This would be no surprise if an overwhelming majority of Indians *were* vegetarian, but the opposite is true. Even government data admits that 70 per cent of the country eats meat and eggs. Independent studies suggest the figure is closer to 80 per cent.[31] Yet, some state governments refuse to serve eggs in the mid-day meals in schools. Meat is not supplied at all, although protein and mineral deficiencies are high. On the other hand, there have been reports from certain schools that meals were discarded because the cook belonged to a scheduled caste.[32] Or, that upper-caste cooks were throwing food onto the plates of lower-caste children so as not to come in contact.[33]

Scheduled tribes and castes, Muslims, Christians, some Buddhists are traditional meat-eaters. Only a few of the upper castes and Jains are 'pure' vegetarian, yet their culture dominates in government-controlled institutions as well as commercial and public spaces.

Where I grew up, in JK Puram, there were a few Jain families. The community is strictly vegetarian with additional taboos against root vegetables, onions and garlic (they are not vegan, however, and dairy products are consumed by all, including monks, who give up all possessions, even their clothing). Around Navratri, a nine-day religious festival, some Hindus also turn vegetarian. As a child, I remember being told by an adult – not a family member – that we must not eat eggs at this time and not leave onion peel outside the kitchen with the garbage, where anyone could see it. This was not management policy in the township. It was an attempt by a powerful minority to control others' food choices.

In Mumbai, every street corner sells a 'Bombay sandwich'. This is a vegetable sandwich. Many stalls also offer a 'Jain' version, minus onions. Jains form 0.36 per cent of the population. Most Indians, especially most Maharashtrians, eat meat. Yet I have never seen a sandwich stall that sells meat and eggs at the same stall as vegetarian sandwiches. I have never seen a vegan stall: the idea of dairy-free food in the public sphere is not just marginal, it is culturally risky. Veganism disrupts the popular rhetoric of cattle being indispensable, and of the consumption of milk making our relationship with bovines maternal rather than merely pastoral.

The oldest Sanskrit texts refer to the eating of beef. However, sometime between 300 BCE and 300 CE there was a shift; Sanskrit texts began to discourage the eating of cow meat.[34] Beef is banned in most Indian states today. Groups that continue to eat beef are among the poorest, least nourished, least equipped to assert cultural rights and, if they do so, are penalised. A college teacher was arrested for writing a Facebook post stating that Santhal Adivasis traditionally ate beef and have a right to continue doing so.[35]

Meat, and by extension, meat-eaters, are expected to retreat from the public arena, or to occupy it gingerly. Political and quasi-political groups feel emboldened to force chicken shops to shut during Navratri, and the administration does nothing to stop them. The new metro rail system in Mumbai involves intense security checks – handbags through scanners and metal detectors – and guards ask passengers to leave if they happen to be carrying meat or fish, no matter how neatly packaged. I know, because I've been asked.

Beef bans have been in force for decades, but in some states the punishment for killing cattle is now more stringent than for assaulting or raping humans. Some politicians want to make it a capital offence. Muslims have been lynched for just transporting cattle, even if they have the requisite paperwork. Some were lynched on video, yet the culprits were acquitted by the court.[36]

In my neighbourhood, a store that sold packaged and semi-processed meats stopped selling lamb, sticking only to chicken. I asked why. No answer was forthcoming. I wasn't really expecting one.

*

Words shape relationships, including one's relationship with oneself. In an article titled 'What Hindi Keeps Hidden', Sagar, a journalist, wondered why his own sociopolitical awakening came so late, and concluded that the answer lay in the literature of a language infused with Sanskrit and Brahmanical impulses. For dominant castes, it was 'a tool to further their varchasv, or dominance'.[37]

The dominant narrative is this: Sanskrit is the mother of all Indian languages. Those of us who grew up in India have heard this repeated often. Sanskrit is not presented as a classical or literary language but as a womb from which 'we' had emerged. And how can a mother be challenged, or abandoned?

The narrative continues thus: Hindi is a derivative of Sanskrit. Hindi is spoken by the largest number of Indians. It must be *the* national language, cleansed of Persian or Turkic words even at the cost of dispossessing its own speakers.

Linguists of repute would disagree that Sanskrit is the 'mother' of all Indian languages. In fact, research suggests that Sanskrit originated in the vicinity of Syria, closer to the cradle of western monotheistic religions.[38] Such research is viciously contested though, for it doesn't fit the dominant narrative.

Urdu is the counter-narrative. It looks like Persian and Arabic, but its foundation is Sanskrit. However, unlike its sibling, it is homeless in the land of its birth. It is the second language of Uttar Pradesh but the intimate destabilisation involved in separating Hindi from Urdu means the latter isn't allowed out of its box, which is labelled 'Muslim'.

Middle- and upper-class Muslims who want a mainstream, viable education for their children send them to English or Hindi medium schools, most of which refuse to teach Urdu. Students at Urdu medium schools are almost exclusively Muslims who have little opportunity to interact with children of other faiths. Urdu newspapers are not subscribed to by English or Hindi medium schools and colleges. Urdu is missing from magazine stands at suburban railway stations, and from airport bookstores.

In recent years, scraps of Nastaliq – the name of an old railway station, the title of a Hindi film – began to catch me unawares, and brought me to the verge of tears. I would think of Grandma: how lost she must have felt despite living in the same country, even the same province in which she was born. She was not an immigrant. Yet, she couldn't read instructions at airports, the names of shops, the prices of things. She wouldn't have been able to read a restaurant menu.

She had her own bank account but depended on others to operate it although she *was* literate. I used to wonder why she never went to the bank herself but I envisage it now: not being able to read the forms she was expected to fill in, tellers getting impatient. How bewildered, how isolated she must have felt outside the house. Probably in the house too, given that she was the only one in our family who spoke no English.

Too late! I learnt to read and write Urdu too late for it to matter. Why did I bother at all?

I learnt partly because, after my grandparents died, I began to visit the graveyard and realised that I couldn't read names on headstones. Each visit, I was assailed by regret (so much left undone! unsaid!) and also a kind of shame about being alienated from my own language. For the first time, I began to think of Urdu as 'mine', not as intimate possession but as intimate loss.

Another rude awakening came one afternoon when I went pamphleteering in Delhi. I was part of a group working on changing attitudes to street sexual harassment. We carried posters and pamphlets in English and Hindi. A small crowd gathered, including bearded and white-capped men who seemed genuinely interested. One of them asked for a pamphlet in Urdu.

I was taken aback. It hadn't occurred to me that we should get pamphlets done in Nastaliq. Shamefully, it hadn't struck *me*, whose grandmother had never been able to read anything else. Pamphlets were printed in languages like Bangla or Kannada in other states. But for Urdu, in the heart of the country where this language had blossomed, we had nothing. I saw then how people are destabilised also through being left out of campaigns and the big conversations unfolding around them, through being made to feel as if they are irrelevant.

I began to learn Nastaliq, complaining bitterly all the while about how much instinct and foreknowledge it demands. I longed for the precision of Nāgri. But my desire to grow intimate with Urdu grew in proportion to the hostility it confronted. In Delhi, a wall art project was defaced because it included a couplet in Nastaliq. A mob had threatened to shoot the artists if they didn't paint it over.[39] Officials at Panjab University have twice attempted to designate Urdu a 'foreign' language.[40] The crowning insult came when two members of the Uttar Pradesh state assembly were denied permission to take their oath in Urdu.[41] Another representative, a municipal councillor, was charged with 'malicious intent of outraging

religious sentiment' for taking his oath in Urdu, and was allegedly assaulted by other councillors.[42]

*

Urdu is claimed as a mother tongue by just over 4 per cent of
India. The Muslim population is over 13 per cent.[43] Clearly,
most Indian Muslims are not intimate with Urdu. The conflation
of language with religion has damaged both.

Those who can still read it are assumed to be Muslim and
treated as if they do not belong. On social media, I noticed a post
from a young woman who was reading an Urdu booklet in the
metro rail; a co-passenger had said things such as 'these people
are Pakistanis'.[44]

I was afraid of similar treatment in Mumbai after I started to
learn Urdu. For a year, each time I felt the nip of fear in my
heart, I documented it.

> *Got nervous reading a marsiya by Mir Anis. The thought crossed my
> mind that if someone gets suspicious, I can show them, because the book
> is bilingual and the facing page has the text in Devnagri font, along with
> word meanings.*

> *Found myself worrying about the 'Ishq Urdu' (Love Urdu) badge that
> I've pinned on my bag. The word* Urdu *is written in Nastaliq. Turned
> my bag the other way while passing security at the metro station.*

> *I was afraid to quote a line from an Urdu poem while doing political
> commentary. I wanted to respond to politicians doing their whirl-
> wind religious tourism campaign by quoting: 'Aise sajdon se Allah
> milta nahin, har jagah sar jhukaane ka kya faayda' (You do not
> attain God by bowing your head at every step). I don't know if that
> would put me in some kind of box labelled 'Muslim' commentator, so
> I left it out.*

> *Deleted WhatsApp messages, a lot of inspirational quotes in Urdu.
> I am travelling to Australia and I don't want to be questioned in case
> I'm picked out for a random check. Can't be seen with anything looking
> like Arabic.*

*I am afraid that if I tweet in Nastaliq, it will mark me out as more Muslim. Those who are watching will not comprehend and people are suspicious of, angry at, the things they cannot comprehend.*

*

When I was little, my grandmother had given me a silver *tabeez* (amulet) inscribed with a verse from the Quran, the Ayat al-Kursi. Grandma said it would keep fear at bay. None of my friends at school ever commented. Amulets were common across faiths. The only reason I stopped wearing it was because the clasp broke and then I put it away and forgot.

I wore it again the year Grandma was dying. I was on my way to see her but en route, I wore the tabeez as an artefact of love, not as an article of faith. Work was taking me through Gujarat, which had witnessed an anti-Muslim pogrom a few years before, in 2002. It was disorienting, how familiar this state felt, even though I had never lived here. I could negotiate the cities easier because I could read the text on signboards and walls. I could also read the subtext. There was hostility and sneers directed at '*miya-bhai*', a local term for Muslims. In the middle of a busy textile market, talking to shopkeepers about migrant workers from Uttar Pradesh, I froze when I realised that the tabeez was still around my neck.

With a subtle gesture, I tucked it out of sight, lest the script give me away as one of 'those people'. People who had been shown their place. People whose homes had been burnt down. Women who had been raped.

The tabeez did not keep fear at bay. For years, I would look at it and the memory of my fear would return, and shame at having to hide a token of my grandmother's love. It took another decade for me to look up the translation of the Ayat al-Kursi. Once I knew what it said, I began to understand why people say that it makes you fearless. I don't wear it much but if I do, I wear it visibly. Because, as much as home is a place of safety, it is also a place where you are visible.

To inhabit a script is to assert one's right to be read, not only by those who are familiar but also those who are not, and thus to be understood. Wherever this right is denied, it forebodes disaffection, even the fracturing of a homeland. Pakistan, for instance, resisted demands that Bangla, used in the eastern provinces, be treated on a par with Urdu. Linguistic hegemony, combined with the political hegemony practised by politicians and army generals in West Pakistan, eventually led to a war that ended with Bangladesh declaring its independence.

Within India too, linguistic conflicts have raged. In Assam, there was resentment of Bangla-speaking outsiders. Being a religious *and* linguistic minority attracts twice as much hostility, so Bengali-Assamese-Muslim was not an identity anyone was anxious to flaunt. It was worn quietly, defensively. Until now.

Nearly a third of the Assamese population is Muslim.[45] Many Bangla speakers chose to list Assamese as their mother tongue to strengthen their claims of belonging. In recent years, however, a new poetic subculture has emerged called Miya (or Miyah) poetry.

*Miya* was originally an Urdu word that meant 'gentleman', but it began to be used as a slur for Bengali Muslims, particularly those who are too poor to mask their identity through dress or education. A group of young Muslims began to write poetry that reclaimed the word. They wrote in multiple languages: English, Assamese and Miya, a Bangla dialect with Assamese infusions. Shalim Hussain, who has been translating and sharing the poems on social media, told an interviewer that each dialect offers a unique worldview. 'There are some things in the real world that standard English, Hindi or Assamese just cannot see. For example, the sound an earthworm makes while crawling through the mud.'[46]

This assertion of their community's unique experience and pain caused an unexpected backlash. Police complaints were

filed against Miya poets, who were accused of posing a threat to
national security. Newspapers suggested that Miya poetry was
a blueprint for the destruction of the Assamese language; television channels debated whether or not the poetry was anti-
Assamese.[47] A senior writer even described Miya as an 'artificial'
dialect.

A lot of heartburn was on account of the poets writing Miya in
the Assamese script. Commentators have pointed out that the
crux of the debate was an expectation that language and literature must serve to preserve the dominant Axomiya (Assamese)
way of life, and that any deviance is seen as treason.[48]

Deviations of script pose a risk because, in rendering a different
worldview into the dominant language, one can force a powerful
group to re-examine itself: is it truly that which it claims to be? Is
this who it *wants* to be? Is there another way of being?

*

English and I are mutual possessions. Perhaps the memory of
Sanskrit's geometrical precision and its accompanying baggage
of invisible rivers also lurks somewhere in my being.
Hindustani was like a mother's heartbeat in a foetal ear. Urdu
was intimate loss.

Even after I recognised how this loss was effected, and what
else I was losing through not learning the script, I held back
from a full embrace. As long as it was intellectual or cognitive
laziness, I could forgive myself, but once I recognised fear, the
loss was no longer acceptable. A beloved needs acknowledge-
ment and shelter, after all, not post-mortem guilt.

Finally, I began to read and write Nastaliq in public spaces.
Finding a seat on the train, focusing on the intimate guesswork
demanded by the script, fighting the temptation to look up to
see if others were staring, setting aside my privileges – being
English speaking, Hindi speaking, dressed carefully – that had
kept me from being identified as 'the other', slowly, I am
becoming the possession of my mother's mother's mother
tongue.

The great crowds in Mumbai had once engendered a rare,
cosmopolitan culture that embraced all migrants.

# 4 THE WANDERING BROTHER

My mother laughs when she recounts how I had urged her to buy a house – anything, anywhere! – because we had nowhere to call our own. Full of adolescent drama, I had said: *I need at least six feet of earth!*

She had spent fifteen years working in two industrial township schools in Rajasthan. She learnt to use a spade and broke rocky ground that no gardener thought could be made to yield. It yielded spider lilies and tube roses. We grew accustomed to the landscape. Quitting or losing the job, however, meant losing the place. It was impossible to belong to a township where you needed the management's permission to stay.

I wanted not just a roof overhead but a roof that couldn't be retracted. A bit of earth that couldn't be pulled out from under my feet.

My mother may have been amused by my drama; nevertheless, she put her life's savings into a small apartment on the fringes of a very big city that was, my brother argued, the only 'city' in the country. The rest of India, he said, was a village.

I scoffed, but there was no denying Bombay's fabled cosmopolitanism. As a port, it had been familiar with sailors and merchants of half a dozen ethnicities including Arabs, Portuguese, British, Abyssinians, Persians. By the nineteenth century, it was India's second largest trading and manufacturing hub. Only half its population was Marathi-speaking, and that half too had migrated from elsewhere.

Bombay wasn't just built by but also *for* migrants. Factories needed hands. Owners, often migrants themselves, helped create basic urban infrastructure. Cheap one- or two-room apartments were built in the heart of Bombay, in what's known as the mill district. People learnt to live with an inherited culture at home and a mixed-up culture outside. The city developed its own patois, Bambaiyya, a street dialect broadly based on Hindi but with infusions of Gujarati, Marathi, Konkani and Dakhani.

Nobody wasted much time dwelling on where you came from; what you were willing to do mattered more. Besides, people knew better than to dwell on antecedents. Pressed up against strangers in a bus or train – groin to groin, nose to armpit – the memory of social distance and hierarchy could only cause paralysis in a country where untouchability was rampant.

By the time we moved, the riots of 1992–93 had dealt a severe blow to the city's cosmopolitan reputation. Thousands were killed, women were raped, Muslim-owned establishments were set on fire. Most politicians did little to contain the violence. The Shiv Sena won the next state assembly elections and changed the capital's name to Mumbai. 'Bombay', it was argued, was a non-native name.

Still, in the popular imagination, Bombay/Mumbai was the city where nobody went to sleep hungry. It would not guarantee shelter but it would give you bread. Writers, actors, software developers, labourers at construction sites, plumbers, carpenters, chauffeurs: all found work.

The city put me through a wring-dryer twice a day before it held out the promised bread. It was unlike anything I'd seen, read or imagined. The longer I traversed its lengths, the more I felt as if the city was scraping off my childhood skin and I wasn't growing a new skin fast enough. But I never had to sleep rough or go hungry.

I paid taxes. I learnt to forgive (a woman who slapped me on the train) and to hit back (men who tried to stalk or humiliate me). If I walked at my natural pace on the street, someone was sure to shove past, muttering 'Garden mein chal reli hai?' ('Taking a stroll in a garden?') A few years later, I was snapping at others who strolled rather than sprinted.

I gave up wearing dupattas after a tangle of impatient commuters nearly strangled me with the one I was wearing. Like other women, I put on scarves only after I got off the train. Like them, I went to the beach to eat snacks rather than to swim. I waded through overflowing drain-water to get to work, even filing reports with my feet on top of a dustbin in a flooded room. The city had one rule – keep going. I kept going. I was even starting to speak in a less grammatically correct Hindi, in keeping with the patois. In short, I became the average Bombayite/Mumbaikar.

Yet, this was also the city where, for the first time, I grew aware that the word *bhaiyya*, 'brother', was not always a term of respect.

Across India, it is common to address strangers as if you are related to them: *Bhai*, *Bhaiyya* or *Didi* for men and women respectively, if they are approximate to your age. It is considered good form everywhere, including Mumbai where Marathi speakers use *Maushi* (aunt) to address women and *Bhau* (brother) for men. *Bhaiyya*, however, was a different matter. It was a word people of north Indian origin, like myself, used, and it became synonymous with Hindi-speaking migrants. We came to embody *Bhaiyya* as outsider.

*

In *India Moving*, Chinmay Tumbe argues, 'If the major ideological battle of the twentieth century was between capitalism and communism, in the 21st century it is likely to be between cosmopolitanism and nativism.'[1] This certainly proved true for India, where nativism had a head start. As early as the eighteenth century, in the southern kingdom of Hyderabad, there was hostility towards northern administrators the ruler was trying to import for their talent. He was pressured into a policy of hiring *mulkis*, or locals, and the official language of administration became Urdu rather than Persian, since Urdu was native and Persian was not.

The Constitution of India guarantees citizens the right to move and work anywhere in the country. However, nativist

movements have emerged to secure jobs for 'locals', interpreted
loosely as someone who speaks the dominant language in
a particular state. Bombay Presidency was split up into
Maharashtra (Marathi-speaking regions) and Gujarat (Gujarati-
speaking regions), with intense squabbling about who would
get Bombay. Maharashtra got to keep it, but the question of who
the city belongs to, and who belongs in the city, still hung in the
air.

There were demands, in the 1960s, that the state stop using
English. With the emergence of a new political party, the Shiv
Sena, the nativist movement grew aggressive. In *Samrat: How the
Shiv Sena Changed Mumbai Forever*, journalist Sujata Anandan
writes, 'Maharashtrians constituted 50 per cent of the population of Bombay (about 40 per cent today), but most were blue
collar workers'.[2] Party chief Bal Thackeray (1926–2012) had
railed against migrants in speeches and editorials, although
his ire was initially directed at south Indians, who were better
educated and took the better jobs. A political cartoonist himself,
Thackeray represented the middle-class south Indian as an
'ugly, grotesque figure' with tag lines such as S.I. vultures.[3]
The campaign against them included the slogan '*Pungi bajao
aur lungi hatao*' ('Blow the horn, remove the lungi'), a thinly
veiled call to attack those who wore lungis (a type of sarong),
as south Indians traditionally did. This, despite the fact that
Thackeray himself wore lungis.[4]

Chinmay Tumbe also shares a story about his father's family
changing their names in the 1960s. While their neighbours
were politically anti-migrant, they were not aggressive. Even
so, an uncle decided to change his name and that of his siblings,
so they would not stand out as south Indians. Traditionally,
a single alphabet letter was used as a prefix or suffix to represent the family's place of origin; he changed 'T' to Tumbe, the
village that the family came from, and used that as a surname
instead because it was phonetically similar to Marathi surnames
like Kamble or Nene.

By the time I moved to Mumbai, the focus of resentment had
shifted. There was intermittent lashing out at non-native

cultural expression. We were warned against celebrating Valentine's Day since it was not a local festival. Commercial establishments were asked to display names in Marathi, or else! Thackeray called for ration cards, which confirm residence and guarantee food at minimum prices for the poor, to be denied to north Indians.

What was ironic about the Shiv Sena's belligerence was that Thackeray's parents too were migrants. A breakaway faction of the party – now the Maharashtra Navnirman Sena (MNS), led by Bal Thackeray's nephew – was aware of this irony and tried to create a false personal history for the family on their website, suggesting that they had moved to the city from within the same state.[5] Questions of origin were pertinent because the MNS was carrying on where the Shiv Sena left off. By 2008, 'Bhaiyyas' who made very little money in the informal economy – street-food vendors and auto-rickshaw drivers – were being attacked.

Earlier, in 2003, the Shiv Sena had initiated a 'Mee Mumbaikar' campaign, seeking to define who was a legit resident. Liberal voices in the party argued that it could be anyone who made a 'contribution', or someone who did not 'milk' the city by not paying taxes. Slum dwellers, 55 per cent of the population compressed into 12 per cent of the city's land, were singled out for castigation.[6] As one Shiv Sena advocate put it: 'Why are you leaving Uttar Pradesh and Bihar? Why are you coming here to live in slums?'

He was asking the wrong question, of the wrong people. Less than 12 per cent of migrants work across state borders in India. Of the 574 million migrants in Maharashtra, the overwhelming majority – 479 million – move within the state, many of them fleeing drought and debt.[7] However, they were not accused of milking the city merely because they were hungry or homeless.

Émigré politicians tap into native sentiments among migrant communities. That north Indians were starting to win elections in Mumbai alerted Marathi speakers to the fact that they couldn't take political power for granted. 'Bhaiyyas' in the city were not wealthy, but they were no longer content with bread and a spot in a slum. They wanted representation, and had started to express themselves through language, food and their worship of the feminine aspect of the sun as a goddess, rather than the locally favoured god.

*

Governments have always attempted to control mobility. Tumbe writes that in the ancient Indian kingdom of Magadh, people had to pay a road toll and immigration was controlled. There were additional rules governing the movements of untouchable castes and married women. As recently as the nineteenth century, there were taboos against overseas travel. Crossing the seas, it was believed, caused you to lose caste. Given that caste is hereditary, it is near impossible to 'lose' unless you change your name and actively shroud your lineage. Metaphorically speaking, however, you could lose caste by travelling to lands where nobody monitored who you touched, or married.

Taboo or not, Indians did travel. Ever since the British started maintaining detailed records, we have data showing that India is one of the most migration-prone nations. Between 1834 and 1937, over 30 million people emigrated, mainly to Burma, Malaysia and Sri Lanka, of which nearly 24 million returned. Over 2 million were taken as indentured labour to British, Dutch and French colonies.[8] Between 1873 and 1916, Suriname alone received 34,000 Indians from the 'Bhojpuri' region: a swathe of districts in Uttar Pradesh and Bihar where Bhojpuri was spoken.

The peasants who went overseas were only following a pattern. In *Cultural and Emotional Economy of Migration*, social scientist Badri Narayan describes it as a 'continuation of the old military migratory patterns'.[9] These emigrants were called Purbias, men from the east, or more accurately, from the eastern districts of Uttar Pradesh and parts of western Bihar.

I looked at Azamgarh district to construct an image of the sort of place that cannot hold onto its people. The district gazetteer of 1921 recorded that about 61 per cent of the local population depended on agriculture. The land was fertile, the climate equable, yet there wasn't enough food. 'In good years there is little or no export, in bad there is considerable import', notes the gazetteer. Conditions could be further judged from the observation that a house of brick or masonry was rare. The economy, even a century ago, was driven by emigration. Between 1891 and 1900, 'no less than Rupees 12 lakh were annually remitted'. At least 76,079 people from Azamgarh alone had migrated to other regions or gone overseas. A century later, the same region still sends workers all over the country, and is still sustained by remittances.

Badri Narayan notes that the lives of the descendants of those who went overseas in the colonial era improved significantly, while the families that didn't migrate remain poor. Other studies also indicate that the probability of remaining poor in India is lower among migrants than among families who do not send at least one member of the family to work outside the village.[10] Poverty often means not having the minimum caloric value needed to stay alive, so we can imagine the consequences of *not* migrating.

Over 454 million of 1.2 billion people, or 38 per cent of India, is a migrant. This is defined by the 2011 census as people born outside the place where they currently live, and probably does not take into account seasonal migrants who return to home base every few months.[11]

North Indian 'Bhaiyyas' go further north, to Kashmir and Punjab, and much further south, to Kerala. As in the era of indentured labour, many of them don't know where exactly they're headed, or where they'll sleep. Many are brought by labour contractors, who respond to a demand for strong and skilled bodies, even in overcrowded cities like Mumbai that pretend not to need them.

*

Hindi film script writer and poet Javed Akhtar once repeated a bit of wisdom that's been handed down by the elders: it takes four generations to create a culture, but only one to destroy it.

Cultural destruction can come from disruptive events like war, earthquakes or famine, mass migration, but it can also come from reactionary nativism and intolerance.

Bombay was an island city but, in a metaphorical sense, it was the opposite of an island. It grew north–south, vertical–horizontal, wresting every inch of space from sky and sea, taking in people from all ten directions. There used to be mock-arguments in India with people taking sides between Delhi and Mumbai. The former represented the landlocked north – more open space, more tangible history, more afford-able housing, but politically rife, unhurried, given to out-bursts of machismo and feudal hangovers, hostile to women. The latter represented west-facing southern port towns – fast, business-like, glamourous, women out in much larger numbers, decent public transport, but also brutal in what it extracted by way of time, space, nuance and personal ideals.

I came as an outsider to both cities, and I saw the truth of both stereotypes. I had moved to Delhi for a few years, partly because I couldn't deal with the petty cruelty and daily panic of Mumbai's overloaded trains, and when I did return, I chose a flexi-work or freelance routine. I needed to feel safe if not comfortable. I also saw both cities change over two decades. Delhi became a bigger migrant hub, with better public trans-port, more complex regional politics. It began to take on some of the nicer aspects of Mumbai, where the infrastructure has not kept pace. There is more muscle flexing, and politics in Mumbai is less about pressing for workers' rights and more about who is, or is not, a rightful resident.

Disruption can also come from technology. One of the nicest things about Mumbai was its web of diverse friendships formed in brief snatches of time. You had 'building' friends, people you played with as a child, and college friends, train friends, office colleagues, walking friends in parks or promenades. You played cards on the train, joined groups to sing hymns or film songs, even bursting into competitive singing across train compart-ments. I cannot say that this forged an inclusive politics, but it did lend the city a patina of inclusiveness. As long as you could share your tiffin with strangers, or sing with them, the sharp edge of nativism was blunted.

Now people barely make eye contact. With cellphones and cheap internet packages, much of the middle and upper classes are locked into a personal cave of media. Nobody knows what others listen to, or read. On streets, in malls, in the foyer of cinema halls, in trains, in elevators, on beaches, conversation is winding down. The culture we are experiencing does not teach us how to talk – or sing – our way out of discomfort.

Cultural disruption, and the resultant disattachment, is magnified in places where discrimination is normalised. Conversely, when it is not challenged over one generation, discrimination itself becomes the dominant culture. A 2018 study by the United Nations Development Programme (UNDP) and the Oxford Poverty and Human Development Initiative examined multi-dimensional poverty in India. Every second person from the scheduled tribes, every third person from the scheduled castes (castes listed in India's constitution as being historically oppressed and discriminated against) and every third Muslim was found to be poor.

Mumbai is still the safest city in the country for women. I look over my shoulder, but not as often as I would elsewhere. But is it possible to feel at home when you are discriminated against? Or, if you are tolerated, are banished to the margins?

My sense of belonging in the city was shaken when I realised that I was a double, or even triple, negative. I wasn't just north Indian, I was single and Muslim.

The 1992–93 riots had cleaved the city through its heart. Communities that had lived cheek by jowl for decades began to segregate. Renting or buying homes became difficult for Muslims. The suburb where my mother bought her first apartment had started out cosmopolitan. People of all faiths and sects were buying in, united by the fact that they were hanging on to the middle-class shelf by the fingertips.

A few years later, a Muslim writer friend was dismayed to learn that he couldn't buy or rent a home in most parts of the city. For years he struggled with real estate brokers. So often was he asking the sad question – 'Are Muslims allowed in the building?' – that his little son had begun to repeat the words.

A lot of housing societies discouraged Muslim buyers and tenants. My own brother discovered that renting apartments was a problem, even in our suburb, and he wasn't even bearded or cap-wearing. I too had real estate agents hanging up on me when I tried moving out of my mom's flat. Unmarried people were not welcome either. It had become one of the bald facts of urban negotiation. Newspaper articles and blog posts were written about discrimination but nothing was done to fix it, although it was a violation of both the Constitution of India and the ethos of the city. Little or no political challenge was mounted by politicians or influential business houses.

The Pew Research Centre indicated in 2010 that the number of global Indian migrants has doubled over the last twenty-five years. As a percentage of the population, the size of the diaspora has not changed, but a disproportionate percentage of religious minorities has been leaving.[12] Christians formed 19 per cent of emigrants though they comprise less than 3 per cent of our population; Muslims accounted for 27 per cent although they comprise about 13 per cent of the population. Whether they are leaving because of uncertainty, poverty or discrimination, is hard to say. Chances are, they face discrimination on the basis of colour or race in their new locations too. However, it is harder when you're treated like a stranger in a place that you've always thought of as home.

My writer friend, born and raised in Mumbai and struggling to rent an apartment here, finally decided to move to another country.

*

Sorrow is the key to home. Without a sense of having lost something, without aching a little, how does one know the strength of one's attachment?

In north India, the concept of *Pardes* (anywhere that is not your native place) is different from *Bides* (foreign lands). Both suggest distance and the likelihood of becoming strangers. In the folk psyche, Narayan writes, overseas migration was a form of imprisonment and exile, as represented by the word *Kala-pani* (black water), an island prison from where escape was near impossible.[13] Yet, many Indians chose to emigrate because to stay was also punishment. It was a choice between devils known and unknown – poverty and discrimination on the one hand, and bondage, loss of identity, loss of beloveds and uncertainty on the other.

For a migration-prone region, pain is embedded in Bhojpuri culture. Badri Narayan writes about '*Bidesiya*' as a cultural genre, both in the homeland and in the émigré's destination. The expression for the ache of separation is '*bidesiya bhav*', and it can be found in music, drama, paintings that speak of loneliness, or of troubles back at home.

People carry what they can to reconstruct home in new places. When people began to leave for the Caribbean as indentured labour, they carried the lightest version possible: faith, language, memory. Folk songs, stories, copies of the Ramayana, Hanuman Chalisa, Quran and Hadiths, poems by Kabir, the sacred thread they wore, souvenirs like a Queen Victoria rupee were passed down to the next generation.[14] They could hold on to their culture partly because they migrated in groups, and partly because they had limited interactions with European plantation owners or native Caribbean populations. Thus, a Bhojpuri migrant in Mumbai, in Suriname, or in Holland could claim similar cultural roots.

After Suriname gained independence, many Indians migrated to Holland, where they were identified as Surinamese-Hindustanis. This time, cultural memory disintegrated faster. Narayan writes that 'wanting to be as Indian as possible, while obsessively holding on to what one originally took with him or her as well as turning away from Dutch culture, led to isolation and a generation gap'.[15]

The sentiment is familiar to migrants all over. Like young Surinamese-Hindustanis, they want to claim a rich cultural heritage but know little about it, especially not what makes it 'rich'. They pick things up from Bollywood films, television soaps, lifestyle magazines. They identify as Indian or hyphe-nated Indian – British-Indian, Indian-American – but have lim-ited experience of heterodox religious practices or regional subcultures. The Purbia, or 'easterner', was so defined, after all, by people in Delhi. The same migrant in Mumbai is a Bhaiyya. Further south, he is 'from the north', and in the United Kingdom he might be '*desi*' or South Asian, indistin-guishable from Pakistanis or Bangladeshis.

The first couple of generations endure upsets: unfamiliar laws, new faces, new languages. Migrant and native struggle to adapt, grasping at straws of memory. But the further people move, the more strands break.

This holds true for internal migrants too. As long as they hope to return to the village, their sense of a specific and unique geographical identity endures. Once the connection snaps, the inner location of self blurs.

This can open the door to monocultures and bigotry. Once people have withdrawn their inner anchor from a specific vil-lage or town, it is easier to shoo them into pens of religious affiliation. Religion offers material refuge and the illusion of stability through never-changing mores and rituals; it also offers a global community to which to belong. In India, this has played out as significant financial support from non-residents for organisations that stress homogeneity and mono-culturalism 'back home'.

The size of our international diaspora is significant[16] – over 25 million – and India is the world's largest recipient of inter-national migrant remittances: over USD 69 billion in 2017, and that's just what's accounted for. Political donations in India are anonymous but one can guess at where some of the funding is coming from based on the fact that the government has report-edly considered allowing non-resident Indians to vote.[17] It is a right and privilege denied to internal migrants in India.

Domestic remittances account for no mean sum, about USD 20 billion. However, the majority of internal migrants are poor and too busy to organise themselves and to insist upon that crucial rite of belonging – voting.

\*

Disenfranchisement is the ultimate way a person can be turned into a stranger: through your country turning stranger on you.

People pushed furthest to the margins – those lacking identity cards or fixed addresses, the displaced and the homeless – struggle to get onto electoral lists. Those who live on the literal margins, near international borders, are also at risk.

Consider the Bengal Presidency – the region spanned what is now three separate nations: India, Bangladesh, Myanmar. People didn't necessarily move, the maps did. Burma was once administered through British India. Nearly 7 per cent of its population was of Indian origin, including Bengalis in the Arakan region who were either brought as workers or acquired as slaves – people now called Rohingya. In 1937, the British began to administer Burma as a separate entity and after it won independence, in 1948, controls over citizenship tightened. The Buddhist majority nation, with its military dictatorship, has been brutally intolerant of the Rohingya, who had little option but to keep trying to cross borders.

Within India, the map changed, again and again. Assam is one of the states whose borders have shifted half a dozen times over the last century, and it has suffered decades of violence on account of a militant demand by indigenous Bodo tribes for a separate state.[18] A fifth of the population was born outside the current borders of the state; one-third speak a language other than Assamese.

Demographic anxieties have been fuelled by electoral politics with campaigns against those who look or sound different, and politicians seeking to evict, or at least disenfranchise, minorities. There is now the Illegal Migrants (Determination by Tribunals) Act, which defines 'foreigners' as those who settled in Assam after 25 March 1971. It was struck down as unconstitutional in 2005, but that didn't prevent the government from implementing a National Register of Citizens (NRC) for Assam in 2017. Those who didn't make the list were put in detention centres. Several people have already killed themselves, fearing loss of citizenship.[19]

In South Asia, where hundreds of millions cannot read or write, where documents are easily lost in floods and people are too poor to maintain bank lockers, and where documents are full of mistakes made by careless state officials, this has been a punitive exercise. The family of a former president of India had not been able to produce adequate paperwork.[20] Foreigner Tribunal hearings have been held hundreds of kilometres away with no more than one day's notice.[21]

The establishment of belonging has been turned into a criminal drama where people are deemed guilty unless they can prove their innocence, and where innocence means error-free documentation. A misspelt name leads to prison.

It is possible to have lived in a valley or on a riverbank for a thousand years without a piece of paper to substantiate you. Papers, however, require an interface with bureaucracy, money, or connections to nudge someone into certifying your presence. Many of us have helplessly raged at suggestions that we pay someone to affirm that we live in the houses we live in, that we are indeed standing before a government employee who can vouch for our existence.

When we first moved to Mumbai, we needed a new ration card as identity proof. Weeks after applying, I failed to get one. There was no explanation, but I was encouraged to seek help from 'agents' who hung around and expected me to fork up some money. Out of a grand sense of loyalty to my nation and unwilling to compromise my own sense of integrity, I refused. There was no rejection of my application but there was no card either. Nothing moved until I happened to mention the problem to someone who was well-to-do and well connected, who mentioned this to someone else, who mentioned it to someone in government. I was given a letter from the food and civil supplies ministry instructing the local office to process my application.

I was a journalist who came from generations of literacy, but I was powerless against a system that needs a steady supply of unofficial grease. Early in my career, I learnt not to be deluded about paperwork. Citizenship depends on the whims of a clerk at the window.

At any rate, no paperwork is ever adequate. Records are easily destroyed or manipulated. When nativist leaders go looking for their 'non', no amount of screaming about roots, grandparents or last century imperialism helps.

*

Once the NRC was compiled in Assam, it turned out that the majority of those who could not prove citizenship were Hindu. Politicians did a quick flip-flop, blaming the verification process, soothing ruffled voters by saying that those lacking documentation would not be deported, then appealing to the Supreme Court to allow more tribunals.[22] The existing list was based on paperwork, hard enough to acquire and protect. What would an alternative registry of citizenship be based on?

There are indications. In 2019, the home minister declared that Hindus, Buddhists, Jains and Sikhs would not have to leave the country, even if they are found to be illegal immigrants from neighbouring Muslim majority nations.[23] Combined with the exercise of identifying alleged foreigners, this means that Muslims alone must worry about being placed in a detention camp, and risk being labelled 'doubtful' citizens on account of something as petty as a name misspelt by a government clerk.[24]

The government has declared that 'foreigner' tribunals will be set up across India and it is no accident that 'foreigner tribunals' were tackled first in Assam, where a third of the population is Muslim. A few electoral points can be gained in each constituency through listing people as D voters; D for 'dubious' or 'doubtful'. There are attempts to ignite similar fears in West Bengal, another border state with a Muslim population of 27 per cent, and Uttar Pradesh, with about 19 per cent Muslims. Detention centres are also being built in states such as Maharashtra and Karnataka, which do not have international borders but where internal migration is high.

At the time of writing, Parliament has cleared a new law, the Citizenship Amendment Act, which allows for citizenship to be granted to refugees or people who claim to be fleeing persecution in neighbouring countries such as Pakistan, Bangladesh and Afghanistan, as long as they are Hindu, Sikh, Parsi, Christian or Jain. Muslims are the only group excluded.[25] The law makes no allowances for people fleeing persecution in other neighbouring states such as Hindu majority Nepal, Communist China, or Buddhist majority Sri Lanka and Myanmar.

The meaning of *foreign* is thus reduced not to passport or ancestry but to exclusions of religion. The homeland, by implication, is not a geography but a faith, and any change thereof is liable to get you tossed into the sea.[26]

Allahabad was the city that came up near the sacred confluence of the rivers Ganga and Yamuna.

# 5  PASSPORT TO IRRECOVERABLE PLACES

My passport says that I am a citizen of India and my place of birth is Allahabad, a place that no longer exists. It is now called Prayagraj.

Allahabad – or Ilahabad, as the natives pronounce it – was home to my maternal grandmother. The city emerged on the banks of the Sangam, the confluence of the rivers Ganga and Yamuna. Millions of people come to witness this confluence. If you rowed far enough into the water, you could actually witness the mingling of distinct streams of water, each a different hue. *Sangam* is also a concept that was spread across the lands watered by these rivers. What was called the Ganga-Jamuni tehzeeb was a confluence of Hindu, Muslim, Christian and other resident cultures, each of them fed by half a dozen streams of thought and ritual.

Allahabad was once called the Oxford of the East. It is no longer called that either. In its rechristening and in the dissolution of its intellectualism is a story of the dismantling of the emotional architecture of one of my ancestral homes.

Prayag was a name for the area around the riverbank where religious mendicants and hermits lived. In the sixteenth century, Mughal emperor Akbar came visiting and, struck by its beauty and serenity, commissioned the creation of a new city called Ilahabas: *bas* ('home') to *ilahi* ('the divine').[1] An alternative story is that there already was a settlement in this region named for Alha, a warrior of the Banafar clan whose heroism is written into ballads that have been sung across the countryside for centuries. Whichever version is correct, a fort was built only after Akbar's visit, and a town sprung up around it.

The area where my family home stands was aligned to the Grand Trunk Road. The dust of civilisations east and west undoubtedly fell off caravans and clung to native limbs and tongues. Still, the town was well described by the word *provincial*. In the mid nineteenth century, the great Delhi poet Mirza Ghalib had dismissed Allahabad as a 'desolation where neither such medicine may be had as befits the ailing nor regard for those of rank'.[2]

If it was not a desolation before, it certainly became one after the uprising of 1857 when Indian soldiers tried to seize control of the fort that had been turned into a military cantonment for the British East India Company. British officials later recorded that even women and children felt 'the weight of our vengeance'.[3] Bholanath Chunder, an Indian observer, wrote, 'To "bag the nigger" had become a favourite phrase of the military sportsmen' and that porter or peddler, shopkeeper or artisan were hurried through a mock trial and made to 'dangle on the nearest tree'.[4]

Nearly six thousand people were executed. It took three months for eight carts to finish taking down the corpses that hung at crossroads and in marketplaces, and the bodies were thrown into the river Ganga without ceremony. Ilahabas was utterly undone.

A new city – given a new inflection by the British so it became 'Allahabad' – was built on the site of eight villages razed to the ground. A high court was established, followed by a university. These developments caused a great spurt of immigration with the need for labourers, servicemen, scholars, lawyers. Among them were my great-grandfather, who worked as a *kotwal* or police official, and his brothers, one of whom was a doctor. The four brothers lived together with their families in a roomy townhouse that is inhabited even now by at least half a dozen branches of the family, each with its independent family unit. When we visit, we spend a whole day just nipping into each uncle or great-aunt's room to say hello, and by the time pleasantries have been exchanged, the sun has gone down.

The town itself seemed, to me, to be resigned to its provincial status. An indecisive, stubborn town, slow to change, quick to temper, mannered but unpredictable. I found myself thinking that it is appropriate somehow that one line of my blood came from here. But where precisely?

Hindi writer Gyanranjan has written, 'the beautiful, affluent, glitzy Allahabad is quite distinct from the poor and crowded older town of the Grand Trunk Road . . . the town has its kitchen on one side, its dining room and drawing room on the other'.[5] I come from the kitchen then, and like all kitchens, it is supposed to be invisible to everyone who can afford not to go there. It is the throbbing heart of the city and is also a ghetto for Muslims, some middle class, many poor.

My mother told me that if I was ever lost in this neighbourhood – and chances were, I *would* be lost in that tangle of lanes – I should just ask for Dr Mustafa's house. He was well known because he treated the poor for free. It felt like a tall claim. Tens of thousands of people live here. Who would remember a doctor who's been dead for decades? But Mom was right. I did get lost, and each time, I'd say Dr Mustafa's name and was directed to the right house.

Three generations later, people remembered. It had filled me with a shiver of pride. Pride enough that the narrowness of lanes or the obvious mess in the 'kitchen' didn't intrude on my identification with the city. I came from that lane, that house, and from women who protected each other.

My mother found herself alone when she was expecting me. Her own family was abroad that year and there was nobody to look after her. So she came to the care of her Khala-ammi (aunt-mom) as everyone called her, in Allahabad. Married to a cousin, Khala-ammi lived in the same house all her life, stepping out very rarely. She did step out when it mattered, though, like going to the hospital for my birth.

Fragile and dignified in all that I saw of her, it was hard to imagine she would ever break into a run. But, Mom says, it was she who had run with a new-born me in her arms when she noticed an untied and bleeding umbilical cord.

It was in this house that I first came upon the unthinkable: women smoking! They smoked cheap *beedis* (tobacco in a leaf) instead of cigarettes, and the sight unsettled every cultural nerve in my little body. I'd run to Mom to gasp. She hushed me: it's a habit from hard times. Hard enough that some members of the family were struggling for food. They had the big house but the boys had no jobs. The women had little formal education. They took on what work they could do from within the house. There were beedi-making units nearby, so they started to roll and a couple of matrons started to smoke.

It is impossible to snap this cord of belonging and memory: the hospital where doctors are not available round the clock, those corridors where I imagine my great-aunt running in a panic, the house where I was swaddled in love since the moment of my birth, where uncles and aunts still look fondly at my face and say *You were this small* . . .

\*

The poet Arvind Krishna Mehrotra has written that Allahabad is the story of dust to dust. Centuries of isolation suddenly gave way to cosmopolitanism. Less than a century later, its cosmopolitan sheen was gone.

The cosmopolitanism of the late nineteenth century was fuelled by immigration, and nurtured by a string of exceptional academics. Many of the men – and later, women – who taught at the University of Allahabad were deeply invested here. Perhaps they attempted to turn the campus, even the city, into an extension of their inner selves.

In her history of the university, *Three Rivers and a Tree*, Neelam Saran Gour describes people who went far beyond lectures and examinations. One professor taught arithmetic but wrote monographs on metaphysical subjects, studied Persian and French literature, and could even coach students on anatomical dissections. Another hired a bungalow to 'house impoverished urchins for whom he engaged a local teacher, and to whom he personally taught English'.[6] Another professor drove around town on cold winter nights, carrying blankets for the homeless. The Institute of Soil Science was the result of a large endowment from a professor who was known to wear patchy coats and haggle over the price of potatoes so he could save up for science. There were courses in painting and music. The English and Hindi departments boasted highly regarded poets and critics.

The university's academic reputation can be gauged from the fact that a physicist of the stature of Schrodinger accepted an offer, though World War II prevented his coming.[7] Teachers were 'figures of awe and glamourous erudition'. Gour's own teacher described a campus where, if you threw a stone, you were sure to hit a celebrity for, 'In the high noon of the Allahabad University, teachers were the celebrities.'[8]

The sun of erudition, however, was setting. Academic standards fell as enrolment rose, thanks to an assumption that a degree would lead to white-collar jobs. As early as 1952, a state-constituted commission recommended that the number of students should never exceed 5,000 when the number was already above 6,000.

The decline was swift and a clear sign was the normalisation of campus violence. It began with freshers being 'ragged' by seniors, leading to 'blue faces, swollen eyes and bleeding noses'.[9] Ragging was often a form of brutal assault but such was the approach to intellectual activity, writes Gour, that writing book reviews was deemed a suitable 'penalty' for students found guilty of ragging.

Another sign was political vacuity and corruption. A prominent academic, Harish Trivedi, recalled his foray into student politics in the 1970s, with hopes of reforming 'the rowdy and lumpen Students' Union, which ... seemed to do little else but call for a protracted and violent strike every year, which culminated in a police lathi-charge, with the University then closing down sine die'. His own election brought him to the sad realisation that students had voted for his caste, and not because they shared his hopes for a better academic culture. He also saw his own helplessness: he couldn't even print a cultural magazine because the budget was embezzled.[10]

By the late 1970s, rifle-toting bikers tore about campus; bombs exploded off and on. The year I was born, the vice-chancellor stayed off campus and under police protection for several weeks. With riot and rampage, clerks beaten, teachers threatened, mass copying during examinations, 1978–81 were 'rock bottom' years. Eventually campus elections were banned. When the ban was lifted, in 2005, the Allahabad High Court again found 'gross violation of rules'. One candidate was murdered. In 2019, raids in a hostel led to the discovery of materials for making crude bombs.[11]

As an extension of the self, the campus was no intellectual home. Idealists and oddball geniuses no longer defined it. There is little room for teachers to express ideas. A Dalit professor was recently forced to leave the city after a mischievously edited video surfaced, where he was saying he doesn't believe in any god. A complaint was filed by a student.[12] Instead of standing up for him, the university administration issued the teacher a show cause notice, seeking an explanation as to why disciplinary action should not be initiated.

*

Our attachment to values, cultural symbols, a memory palette is expressed as belonging to a city. A familiar landscape is frozen as a fridge magnet: a bridge, old hand-painted signs, comfort food, poetry. But what if a city is scrubbed of the very things that defined it?

In *The Future of Nostalgia*, Svetlana Boym writes that contrary to intuition, the word *nostalgia* comes not from poetry or politics but from medicine. It was studied as a sickness among soldiers, dangerous enough to warrant treatment through leeches, warm hypnotic emulsions, opium and, of course, a return home. Symptoms included confusing real and imaginary events, hearing voices, seeing ghosts. However, Boym writes, 'Nostalgia is not always about the past, it can be retrospective but also prospective. Fantasies of the past determined by needs of the present have a direct impact on the realities of the future.'[13]

I have little nostalgia for Allahabad. Certainly, I am not sick for it. But I am nostalgic for its shadow future, for the place it could have become, and for the person I could have been if only the university had continued being the Oxford of the East. I longed for campuses filled with the glamour of erudition, for teachers who set ethical standards as high as academic ones. I longed for that time and place Gyanranjan describes, when people's faith in poetry was 'second only to their faith in the heaven-bestowing properties of the water of the Ganges, which they put into the mouths of the dying'.[14] This is a fantasy of a past in which I would have been right at home.

Alok Rai, another scholar from Allahabad, has written that meaning is a conspiracy – 'conspiracy *with*, or conspiracy *against*' – and it is so with names.[15] Allahabad was not renamed as much as it was unnamed. There was no reclaiming of a native name. 'Calcutta' reverted to its native pronunciation, 'Kolkata'; 'Bangalore' went back to 'Bengaluru'; 'Bombay' changed to 'Mumbai', allegedly because it was a foreign name. But 'Allahabad' was not restored to 'Ilahabas', or even to 'Alhabas'. The choice of 'Prayagraj' as a new name points to a conspiracy, to a form of retrospective nostalgia for a past that did not include Muslims.

The city was being recast in a monocultural mould. The religious Kumbh fair, held once in twelve years, has always been a large affair drawing hundreds of thousands of visitors. The last *ardh-kumbh* (a half-cycle fair held every six years) was heavily advertised; over 120 million were expected and a reported 220 million visitors showed up, with great pollution the result.[16]

There was no concurrent attempt to salvage the university, or to create new cultural landmarks that were inclusive. Instead, places named after Muslim rulers were targeted: a railway junction called 'Mughal Sarai' was named for Deen Dayal Upadhayay, a Hindutva ideologue and a divisive figure. Faizabad, the former capital of the province, had its name changed to 'Ayodhya', an ancient kingdom associated with

Ram, who is worshipped as God and in whose name much violence has been unleashed upon Indian Muslims. 'Ayodhya' was already the name of a neighbouring town, which houses the destroyed Babri mosque. Hindutva outfits claim the mosque was built on top of a temple, of which there is no archaeological evidence. There are hundreds of other Ram temples in Ayodhya, but the aim was spelt out in the slogan: '*Mandir Vahin Banaayenge*', 'We will build a temple *there*'. On the same spot where the mosque stands. A decades-long argument in the Supreme Court concluded with the judgement that even though the demolition of the mosque was illegal, a temple should be built in its stead.[17]

There is no archaeological answer to if and when Lord Ram lived, much less the exact time and location. Everyone understands this, including those who destroyed the mosque. The destruction was erasure, just like with the city names. Further down the same road are veiled threats targeting mosques in other towns like Kashi and Mathura.[18]

Muslim self-expression has been challenged through direct violence, as in the case of a teenager who was beaten to death in a train for no ostensible reason other than that his cap and his name gave away his social identity,[19] and also through the sort of chicanery attempted by a member of Parliament who alleged that mosques were 'mushrooming on government land' and submitted a list of fifty-four mosques and graveyards in his West Delhi constituency. The Delhi Minorities Commission visited all fifty-four structures and found none to be illegal. In fact, one of these was a mosque that the MP's own father, a former chief minister, had helped construct.[20]

Svetlana Boym has written of conspiracy as 'an imagined community based on exclusion more than affection'. The unnaming of Allahabad and the false-naming or demonisation of Azamgarh is part of this conspiracy. It seeks to erase our collective memory of Indian Muslim rulers as builders, aesthetes, administrators, and of our home towns being sites of synthesis and confluence. For Indian Muslims, such erasure is an assault upon their inner homeland. It makes them feel unseen, unheard, unremembered. It also erases the memory of the reason so many Muslims were so successful as rulers in India.

Culture is a slippery, fluid thing, but powerful elites like to bolt everyone down in their respective positions – victor, loser, ally, subordinate – by erasing all evidence of fluidity. Racism and slavery operated on similar models, as does the caste system. People have always changed religion to combat hierarchies. In ancient India, they turned to Buddhism and Jainism. In the medieval era, they adopted Islam, Christianity or Sikhism, either to escape caste or to align themselves with the faith of more powerful kings. Part of the work of restorative nostalgia in India is a punitive erasure of these movements.

The word for reconversion to Hinduism is *shuddhi*, or 'purification'. Another term is *Ghar wapsi*, or 'homecoming'. The words are meant to suggest that Muslims and Christians have strayed from 'home' and must be brought back. One way of doing this is to incentivise Hinduism by accepting, at least in theory, that caste-based untouchability is outdated. Another way is to make the country a hostile place for minorities. Demolishing mosques, attacking missionaries, renaming cities are all part of the latter approach. Besides, there are attempts at new laws to forbid religious conversion. Once again, people are being bolted down into their respective social positions.

*

*Sangam* is one of my favourite words. It isn't an object or monument. It is an embrace between fluid entities. It is a veneration of flow itself, of mingling without fear of losing yourself. That this was a way of life for millions of people in north India is evident, even now, if you look closely at the map.

This year, driving towards the Sangam, I turned to Google for navigation support. The map unfurled like a hoary djinn speaking for the city of my birth. Around the confluence were scattered a dozen pinpoints of spiritual diversity: Tikarmafi Ashram, Ma Sharda Mandir, Shiv Mandir, Jhusi Dargah Shah

Taqiuddin, Mazaar-e-Pak Hazrat Ali Murtaza, Murad Shah Baba Mazaar Shareef.

I took a screenshot as a souvenir, uncertain that these names, or even the physical sites, would survive. Uncertain what else would be lost.

I used to adore Prayag. I had once taken a boat out to the point where the rivers meet and allowed myself to be brow-beaten by a Pandit who hung about insisting that I couldn't possibly not need his services, so what if I wasn't quite Hindu? I allowed him to float lamps and flowers in my name, and paid him. None of it felt unnatural.

The spiritual fluidity of India is one of the things that gives me balance. It is natural for most of us to be devoted to our own traditions, but also to be open to other spiritual pathways. Hundreds of millions go to temples and dargahs and churches. They would not immerse themselves wholly in the rituals of the other, but would brush against other sacred norms in the belief that piety was piety, no matter where it came from. I myself visit any sacred place that doesn't shut me out. It only strengthens what I have.

I revel in the wisdom of symbolic adjustments made by spiritual masters of yore so that many more might feel included. It is common to see images of Mother Mary draped in a saree, or a Sufi dressed in saffron, as the saint of Deva Sharif did. Or it could be a man dressed always in a bright pink kurta and black cap, and smoking cigarettes, who occupied the seat of leadership at a *dera*, a spiritual residence, devoted to Panj Pir in Amritsar where you'd find images from the Hindu pantheon alongside Machhli Pir, who is also Zinda Pir, or Jhulelal or Khwaja Khizr.

I had once stopped at a tiny roadside shrine in Amritsar, Punjab. It was the tomb of a Muslim Sufi saint, Pir Baba Nupe Shah, and contained objects similar to *alams*, decorative replicas of the standards carried to the battlefield by Imam Hussain. It also contained pictures of Hindu gods. I put questions to the men who took care of it. They weren't sure what they were devoted to. All they knew was that it was a holy place. One of the men had a tattoo on his forehead. He got it at a religious fair in Rishikesh.

Hindu sadhus had asked him to get a tattoo of a crescent moon instead of an Om, so that he may not lose his connection with the spiritual tradition he came from. The man had a Hindu name. Or perhaps he had adopted one. Who knew? Who cared? He'd found a place and a practice that suited his needs.

It is into this confluence that I was born but, like the rivers Ganga and Yamuna, the mix and flow of our lives is dammed up and polluted to the point of toxicity.

I catch myself wondering these days whether Azamgarh too will cease to exist, as Allahabad and Faizabad have disappeared from the map of my times. Its loss of name would stick in my throat like a fish bone. The loss of Allahabad does stick in my throat.

Perhaps what A. K. Mehrotra had said is true – dust to dust. That's the story of this place. I look at the riverbank with tired eyes. It is bald of forest cover. Religion is fine. Surely, there could also be gardens, benches, trees, cafés, art installations? But no. Nothing.

Sometimes I think about 1857 and wonder if, when houses are razed, restless spirits are released. Perhaps there are ghost trees, strung with the spirits of six thousand natives. Perhaps ghost carts do the rounds, cutting down rebels hung at cross-roads. Perhaps it is a curse. The wealthy always scrambling to buy up their lives. Sacred rivers choked and emaciated.

Gyanranjan wrote that he tried to kill the Allahabad within, because it was impossible to have two lovers: 'Ultimately, Allahabad took leave of those who had left Allahabad.' But what happens to those who never left, yet found that the city they knew was gone?

I hear muted sighs, sardonic laughs from lifelong residents. Someone says, the High Court isn't named for Prayagraj yet. Someone else says, it is rumoured that the High Court itself is leaving town. Someone clings to a shred – the university is still Allahabad – but nobody believes that it will remain. Nobody says, what's in a name?

I wonder, when I get my passport updated next, should I say that I was born in Prayagraj? Can I swear to it and put my signature on it, that this is the truth to the best of my knowledge?

The Partition of India was a horrific event and the aftershocks continue to reverberate across the subcontinent.

# 6   MIXED BLOOD

My mother says, wherever you can trace your bloodline, that place is yours. Yours as much as anybody else's. By that measure, the province of Uttar Pradesh is flecked with my blood. Not just Uttar Pradesh, and not just India. Pakistan too.

My history is wrapped up with the history of the Indian subcontinent. Mom is Muslim, from the Indian side; Papa was Punjabi Hindu from the Pakistani side. The border between these two countries is an actual bloodline. The wound of millions being killed and displaced during the Partition is scratched raw every few years through fresh hostilities. Three wars have been fought, skirmishes and shelling continue, accusations of cross-border infiltration are hurled.

India and Pakistan do not give each other tourist visas. Many airlines don't run direct flights. I've even had brows raised at the post office when I tried to send books across the border. When citizens critique their governments, they are accused of being RAW or ISI agents, our respective spy agencies. In India, there is a new trend of rebuking all critics of government policy thus: *Go to Pakistan!*

A former member of Parliament caused a stir ahead of the 2014 general elections when he declared that those opposed to his party's prime ministerial candidate would have go to Pakistan.[1] Another former MP had said that people who want to 'lecture on secularism' can go to Pakistan.[2] The chief minister of Goa declared, 'Go to Pakistan if you want to celebrate it',[3] and one serving minister announced that people opposed to the abrogation of Article 370, which grants special status to the

state of Jammu and Kashmir, should go to Pakistan.[4] When
a bureaucrat resigned his position in protest, an MP called him
a traitor and said he should go to Pakistan.[5]

Wars have heightened the perception that Pakistan equals
the enemy. However, nobody says *Go to China!*, even though
India has fought a war with China and border disputes continue.
Nor is *Go to Pakistan!* similar to *Go back to where you came from!*
Rarely is anyone asked to go to Afghanistan, or Iran, or Iraq, or
Mongolia.

A curious nationalism is being enacted whereby many
Indians define themselves *against* Pakistan. It is as if their
inner location is on the wrong side of the border, their most
intense emotions rooted in estrangement.

To understand this inverted location of belonging, one has to
recall South Asia's recent history of intimate violence and our
mixed genetic heritage. In 1947, British India was divided on
east and west flank. Partition is often written with a capital 'P' to
emphasise the disruption it caused. Over 17 million were
yanked out of their soil abruptly.[6] On the east, about 700,000
left and 2.5 million Bengali Hindus came to India.[7] On the west,
about 6 million Muslims left and 5 million Hindus and Sikhs
came to India.[8] An estimated 2 million died in the accompanying violence. Princely states along the western border such as
Alwar, Bharatpur,[9] and Jammu and Kashmir also saw extreme
violence against Muslims with hundreds of thousands being
killed or displaced.[10]

A sense of displacement accompanied not only those who
left, but also those who stayed. Places where large groups of
refugees settled, changed overnight. In Delhi, by 1951, every
third person was someone from across the border.

Dislocation can be abrupt but the internal compass dissolves
slowly. For months, even years, refugees remain invested in
places left behind. The generation that moved in 1947 was
sharply aware of the contours of its lost home. Intizar
Hussain, often described as a novelist of Partition, writes not
about a nation state but about households, fields, farm workers,
the stillness of summer afternoons, uprooted men seeking

comfort in a refugee language. It took decades for the image to fade and for delicate shades of aesthetic and emotional attachment to dissolve into a general sense of rupture.

My father's family escaped the bloodshed. They lived in Lahore but some of the family had been on the Indian side, holidaying in the summer of 1947. They never went back. My paternal grandfather had to leave his home and business, and start afresh in Delhi and Punjab. I never had a chance to ask what home meant to him. My paternal grandmother had died before my parents even met, and my grandfather died before the wedding. My father too died before I could build a relationship with him. I never heard their stories. No artefacts were handed down to me. Pakistan did not translate into loss, not through my father. However, I did hear stories of loss on my mother's side.

Two each of Grandpa's and Grandma's siblings left for Pakistan. They could meet less than a handful of times in the last few decades. Two of them came to India, separately, very late in their lives. Both died during the visit and were buried here. Whatever place they may have thought of as 'home', it was inevitable that others would say, they came home in the end.

Attia Hosain, in her novel *Sunlight on a Broken Column*, describes a Muslim family divided over their choices during Partition. A character who intends to stay in India says, 'Can you imagine every time we want to see each other we'll have to cross national frontiers? Maybe even have to get visas.' His brother, who intends to leave for Pakistan, laughs, saying, 'there is no need to be as dramatic as all that. Visas indeed!'[11]

I'd laughed out loud when I came upon that passage. There are few bits of paper more difficult to obtain than a visa between India and Pakistan. At literature and cultural festivals, invited guests have not been granted visas. At various times, India–Pakistan cricket matches have been disrupted. Both nations have tried to restrict cultural exchange, like Pakistan banning Indian movies or Indian organisations threatening filmmakers who hire Pakistani talent.

The most tragic aspect of Partition was that most people were clueless as to what the splitting of a homeland entails. Journalist

Saeed Naqvi was privy to family discussions about how the
demand for a new nation state had played out among the
Muslim elite. 'Membership of the Muslim League was
a bargaining tactic used by Taluqdars and big landlords. They
did not want to give up their palaces and their lifestyle,' he
writes in his memoir *Being the Other*. 'Pakistan was never the
goal; it was a bargaining chip.'[12]

There are tragicomic stories about men being enthusiastic
about the idea of Partition but not wanting to leave themselves.
In *India Wins Freedom*, one of the most prominent national leaders, Maulana Abul Kalam Azad, writes of the confusion of the
times: 'these Muslim Leaguers had been foolishly persuaded
that once Pakistan was formed, Muslims, whether they came
from a majority or a minority province, would be regarded as
a separate nation and would enjoy the right of determining
their own future'.[13]

Many of those who voted for Partition had actually voted to
retain the sociopolitical freedoms that they interpreted as
a homeland, which, in their heads, was physically located wherever they lived! Maulana Azad rightly called the situation ridiculous, but it was also unbearably sad.

The leadership on either side did little to explain the consequences or dangers of a demographic split. On the contrary, they
saw minorities as mutual hostages. Azad recalled, 'it was being
openly said in Congress circles that Hindus in Pakistan need not
have any fears as there would be four and a half crores of Muslims
in India and if there was any oppression of Hindus in Pakistan,
the Muslims in India would have to bear the consequences'.[14]

And they did. They still do.

*

I have a persistent suppressed memory. A little girl in school
uniform telling me that I was Pakistani, and me denying it.

Even as a child, I knew there was no argument that could
reach her. What could I say except, no, I am Indian? How much
I am troubled by it can be assessed through how often I try to

forget this moment. Then, I read similar accounts about other children and there it is again: the pretty face, the child's tight knowing smile, and her insistence, *I know you people are Pakistani.*

She had no idea about my father's Punjabi Hindu origin. Her sense of me being Pakistani came from my Muslim surname. I grew up thinking this sort of experience was mine because we lived in a remote township where people didn't know any better. Later, I discovered that it was common to many Indian Muslims, including those who went to college in cities known for their multiculturalism, like Lucknow. Journalist Seema Mustafa writes in her memoir *Azadi's Daughter* that the communal campaign in India has based itself on the violence and ignominy of Partition, and an insistence on linking Muslims who chose to remain in India with Pakistan. The demolition of the Babri mosque in 1992 was another turning point. People no longer asked whether she was Pakistani. Instead, she recalls being flooded with calls threatening to kidnap her and demands that she go to Pakistan.[15]

Saeed Naqvi has also written of a video tape made around the time of the demolition of the mosque. It showed *kar sevaks* (volunteers) threatening to bomb Pakistan and Bangladesh, and a politician saying, 'Muslims can go to Pakistan if they like.' Neither volunteers, who were supposedly there to build a temple, nor their leaders talked of Lord Ram or their personal faith. What was on display was 'a compulsive obsession with Pakistan'.[16]

'Go to Pakistan' has been said so often now, it has turned into a joke with people pointing out that they'd be willing to go if visas were granted. Less funny is the impact on civilians. Muslim children have been coming home crying, reporting that they're called Pakistanis by other kids.[17] More worryingly, unprovoked violence[18] has been unleashed upon Indian Muslim families, with demands that they go to Pakistan.[19]

Maulana Azad had pointed out as early as the 1960s that the creation of Pakistan had only exacerbated hostilities between Hindus and Muslims, for their mutual enmity was given a permanent constitutional form.[20]

Ironically, some of those who tell people off by asking them to go to Pakistan, as if it was on another planet rather than in the neighbourhood, are also given to asserting rights over its territory. Hindutva groups have expressed ambitions for 'Akhand Bharat', undivided India.[21] Looking at some of the unspecific maps floating about the internet, this would include not only Pakistan and Bangladesh but Nepal, Bhutan and parts of Afghanistan and China. Just as the proponents of Partition had no idea what it would actually translate into, proponents of Akhand Bharat have a very sketchy idea of what an undivision would entail, but politicians have spoken of it as a goal.[22]

*

Sometimes I want to respond to *Go to Pakistan!* by crying out, *How dare you! My father's family had to leave Pakistan in 1947, thanks to two-nation enthusiasts like you! I belong here more than you do.*

I don't say it, though. I don't want to make any claims upon India through appeals to Hindu ancestry. The stronger claim is that of Muslims who chose not to leave when presented with a choice. Resisting majoritarianism, I genuinely believe, is the highest form of patriotism. Besides, it is hard for me to identify with my paternal ancestry.

The Lahore roots do not run deep. My paternal grandfather's birthplace was listed as Khanpur and there is more than one village or town called Khanpur on either side of the border. Who knows where that bloodline leads? I have not gone looking for it because I was so comfortably rooted in India on the strength of unstinting love on my maternal side. There was never any question of not belonging, either in the land or in the faith.

The only question that troubles me is this: was Partition concluded in 1947, or was it initiated?

The two-nation theory says that Muslims and Hindus are two peoples and do not belong in the same nation. As long as this theory is not put to rest, the ghost of Partition hovers.

Over seven decades, Indian Muslims countenanced shrinking political visibility, harassment and violence through riots or anti-terror operations. A 2006 report prepared by a committee headed by retired judge Rajinder Sachar on the social, economic and educational status of Indian Muslims found that Muslims did face harassment, with men wearing beards or a *topi* being randomly picked up for interrogation from public spaces like parks, railway stations and markets.[23]

Equally damning was infrastructure and exclusion data. The literacy rate for Muslims was 59 per cent, significantly lower than the national average of 65 per cent. About 25 per cent of kids had never been to school, and the dropout rate was dramatically higher: only 17 per cent Muslims made it to high school, just over 3 per cent were graduates in 2004/05. The General (upper-caste Hindu) percentage was over 15 per cent.

Muslim unemployment rates were also higher than the General, but their share in casual work was higher. Where they did find regular work, they were getting lower salaries in both public sector and private sector jobs. At public sector firms, Muslims comprised about 7 per cent of employees, and their participation in security- and defence-related jobs was the lowest. Muslim workers in security agencies were limited to just over 3 per cent while Hindu upper castes accounted for over 52 per cent.

A large proportion of Indian Muslims work in their own enterprises; many are roving street vendors. What makes success harder is that their neighbourhoods tend to lack infrastructure such as tarred roads and bus stops, which are critical for self-employed people. Over 16 per cent of the villages without any medical facilities were found to be located in Muslim concentration areas. Muslims, scheduled castes and tribes lived in the largest number in villages categorised as 'least electrified'. Only one-quarter of rural households had access to tap water, but Muslims had the least access.

The mean per capita expenditure for India in 2004/05 was INR 712 (about USD 10), but there were great variations. For Hindu-General, this was a mean of INR 1023 (USD 14), for Muslims, INR 635 (USD 9). The figure was lower yet for scheduled castes and tribes. The incidence of urban poverty was highest, over 38 per cent, for Muslims.

There have been riots every few years, and pogroms that could not have been undertaken without the support of at least some public officials. Afterwards, there has been scant justice for victims despite brave testimonies. Supreme Court lawyer Menka Guruswamy has argued that India's refusal to commemorate the violence of Partition has resulted in moral black holes that help to perpetuate it. She writes,

> the impunity that characterised the long process of loot, rape and murder that is Partition has continued to replay itself, to lesser degrees both in form and substance. For instance, the 1984 killing of Sikhs in Delhi, and the 1993 and 2002 butchering of Muslims in Mumbai and Gujarat respectively, are illustrations of the replications of the degradations witnessed during Partition.[24]

Remembrance is essential before people can reflect. Nations that are serious about not repeating genocide make it a point to remember. As Guruswamy points out, many European countries punish Holocaust denial and it is impossible to travel through Germany without coming upon some commemoration of the murder of Jews. The more India and Pakistan try to move on without addressing the causes and horrors of Partition, the lesser equipped we are to prevent fresh horrors.

To look Partition full in the face, we must think about intimate betrayal: neighbour turning on neighbour, employees turning on employers, families killing daughters or asking them to commit suicide rather than risk abduction. But we cannot countenance such betrayals until we stop betraying. Far too many Indians continue to betray the trust of those who are most vulnerable to them, starting with children.

As in Nazi Europe, there remains in the subcontinent an obsession with 'pure' blood and genetic segregation, which is emphasised through physical segregation, such as not allowing tenants from certain religions and castes. Ideas of social pollution are a thin disguise for the real purpose: control of blood and womb.

Modern science shows that the idea of purity/pollution is ridiculous. Our mix of language, food, attire, music, polity pales in significance when we consider genetic evidence that *Homo sapiens* mated with Neanderthals, possibly other *Homo* subspecies.

Within the Indian subcontinent, too, there is ample evidence of mixed blood but there is also a thorny debate about 'purity', since bloodlines are linked to claims over territory and natural wealth. Tony Joseph's *Early Indians: The Story of Our Ancestors and Where We Came From* waded into the debate with archaeological and genetic research to link Sanskrit-speaking Aryans with Steppe pastoralists in Europe and west Asia. There is evidence that Aryans and Dravidians – ancient north Indians and ancient south Indians – were distinct peoples who ended up mixed. DNA studies also suggest that most northern migrants were male. Or else, Aryan females were not permitted to mate with the 'other'. Thousands of years and mixed bloodlines later, our maternal DNA is overwhelmingly southern or non-Aryan. This would suggest that either the Aryans came as invaders, or that gender and racial inequality was already built into their social imagination.

Our civilisational memory runs very deep. Barriers to mixing have been in place for over two thousand years. Joseph writes of a dramatic reduction in genetic mixing around 100 CE, as if 'a new ideology had gained ground and power ... It was social engineering on a scale never attempted before or after, and it has succeeded wildly.'[25]

This was long before Christianity or Islam arrived, so the obvious inference is that caste was being reinforced and power being concentrated. The wild success Joseph refers to is revealed as Steppe ancestry or 'Aryan' genes being most prominent in Brahmins, who are at the top of the caste pyramid. Brahmins were associated with priestly functions, and with Sanskrit texts like the Dharmshastras and the Manava Dharma Shastra or Manusmriti, estimated to have been written before the third century BCE, which prescribe punishments for inter-caste sex.

Shudra men, in the fourth caste, were to be punished with castration for sex with 'unguarded' women of higher castes; if a woman had a guardian – father or husband – the man's punishment was death. Brahmins were rarely given the death penalty; even kings were forbidden from killing them. Brahmin men who raped a 'guarded' woman of equal status were to be fined, but marriage or sex with an outcaste caused the Brahmin to lose his caste.

Segregation was enforced through marriage while girls were too young to conceive or choose mates. The ideal marriage pre-scribed in the Manusmriti is one where the bride is 8 years old if the groom is 24, or 12 years old if the groom is 30. This was the accepted norm, especially in Brahmin households until the end of the nineteenth century when, acting on the petitions of Indian social reformers, the British government intervened. The flash-point was 1889, when an 11-year-old called Phulmoni died after being raped by her husband. In 1891, the minimum age of con-sent, even within marriage, was raised from 10 years to 12.

Nearly a hundred and thirty years have passed since Phulmoni was raped to death, but marital rape is not illegal in India. Child marriage also continues. UNICEF data suggests that one-third of the world's child brides are in India.[26] Our own census admits that at least 7 per cent of all married girls are underage.[27] However, in 2018, one of our lawmakers described the minimum age limitation on marriage as a 'disease'.[28] He said it in the context of young people 'straying', that is, marry-ing into different communities.

The stakes are very high. Genetic segregation helps maintain a slave-like class that cannot claim equality by claiming to have the same blood and bone. The more mixed our blood, the more difficult it is to reject or enslave another set of people.

Mixed marriage is the antithesis of segregation and hier-archy. Those who are invested in preserving hierarchies fero-ciously resist mixing. Matrimonials are advertised along with caste and clan specifications, even in the internet age.

Compliance is ensured through intense scrutiny of relationships, informal caste councils, gender segregation in schools and, when all else fails, violence.

It is not uncommon in contemporary India to have people comment on mixed blood as inferior or somehow tainted. Where disapproval had once meant risking excommunication, now it means risking murder and imprisonment. Couples are hounded, dragged to court, blackmailed with the threat of riots breaking out and causing the deaths of other innocents. The bogey of 'Love Jihad' has been raised across the country, wherein boys are accused of seducing girls for the sole purpose of converting them to Islam. Parents have been known to torture daughters, and even to declare them mentally unfit in a court of law.[29]

I used to collect news reports of 'honour' killings or suicide pacts between lovers, which appeared in the newspapers with depressing regularity:

> *July 2016. Haryana. Girl of 19 locked into a cow dung store, which is then set on fire.*

> *September 2016. Teenage couple elopes. They go to Agra and take pictures of themselves against the backdrop of beautiful historic monuments. They visit the Taj Mahal, widely known as a monument to love. Afterwards, they throw themselves in front of a train.*

> *April 2017. Elderly couple beaten to death by a mob because their grandson eloped with a girl. Boy Dalit. Girl Hindu, backward caste but higher up the scale than Dalit.*

> *March 2017. A boy of 19 and a girl of 18. Different religions. They leave home, get down at a railway station. They hug. Boy shoots girl in the head, then he shoots himself.*

> *February 2017. A couple is found hanging from ceiling fans in a room in Nagpur. Different religions. They were trying to persuade their families to accept the relationship. No suicide note. Cops register a case of 'accidental death'.*

> *March 2018. Kerala man kills daughter on the eve of her wedding. Hindu, upper caste. Boyfriend was Dalit.*

*July 2019. Dalit man beaten and slashed with swords by upper-caste wife's family. She was pregnant. He went prepared, with a women's helpline team, and a female constable. It didn't help.*

I scanned the reports for more detail, something that would make these lovers flesh and blood, something more than the sum of age, caste, religion. In death, at least, they should be seen as something bigger than the ideas that killed them. But most media reports offered no more detail than community and official cause of death. They were buried on the inside pages, in small font.

*

A decade ago, if you were willing to brave the consequences, you could elope. It was possible to start afresh elsewhere. With new tech surveillance, it is near impossible. Your location is given away by your phone or CCTV cameras. The government has pushed aggressively for biometric linked identity cards. Citizens are asked to link biometric data with bank accounts, phone networks and welfare benefits. Jobs, home rentals, driving licences, colleges, hospitals, birth and death certificates – all require a card that would betray you to those who want to kill you.

In July 2019, a video surfaced where the daughter of a politician, an elected member of the Uttar Pradesh state assembly, was asking her father to call off his men.[30] She asked the state to protect her and her husband, who is from another caste, but she chose to do so via social media instead of going to the police.

She could not vest her hopes in the state machinery from which her father derives his power. Instead, she turned to her compatriots, seeking safety in our collective witnessing. The eyes watching, the ears listening, the hearts that may be moved by her plight. Even if we could not protect her, we would at least remember her love and her courage. At least we would know that she had not been kidnapped or raped or killed by her own boyfriend, in case that was the story her family chose to spin.

This was a rare event, though. A desperate move by a desperate couple. Much more common is the ordinary, everyday harassment couples face in public and in private.

Instances of citizens being assaulted for being out with a member of another community are rarely documented. Unless, of course, they are documented by the perpetrators themselves. In 2015, in Mangalore, a coastal town known for its distinctive tiles and its fiery seafood, a man was stripped naked, tied to an electricity pole and assaulted in full public view by a Hindutva group called the Bajrang Dal. We were duly informed that the man was Muslim, and the woman, Hindu: the victim had taken a colleague out for a drive because he'd just bought a new car.

The Bajrang Dal was unapologetic. Its members have been accused of – nay, have boasted of – kidnapping girls who marry outside their castes and communities, breaking their spirit, then 'purifying' them and getting them re-married to some other man.[31] The group is not one of its kind; others like the Sri Ram Sene and the Hindu Yuva Vahini have also begun to attack couples. From public space, assaults have moved into private rooms. Vahini members reportedly barged into an apartment and assaulted a couple.[32] They had no fear of the law. In fact, it was the attackers who dragged the couple to the police station, rather than vice versa.

These developments appear to me as a grotesque inversion of Partition, when both Hindu and Muslim girls were kidnapped by the other community and turned into captive wives. Now girlfriends and wives are being kidnapped, assaulted, and turned into captive wives by their own families. After Partition, the state worked with activists to rescue kidnapped women. Now the state seems unwilling to act against 'activists' who kidnap women.

*

There was a time when Indians who wished to marry across religious lines had to either formally convert, or declare themselves atheist, or go to Switzerland to solemnise the union. Eventually the Special Marriage Act of 1954 regulated interfaith unions through registration, known in common parlance as a 'court marriage'. However, couples must declare their intention thirty days in advance via a notice at the district court. The marriage officer is required by law to enter such notices into a marriage notice book, which can be seen, free of charge, by anyone.

Thirty days is the long gap between hope and death. There has been no change in this provision despite frequent reports of families killing interfaith couples.

In early discussions leading up to the drafting of the Indian constitution, the question of consent at the time of marriage was raised. One of the leaders of India's independence movement, Princess Amrit Kaur, had argued that the right to consent ought to be enshrined in the constitution. She was out-argued.

The Constitution of India has been amended 103 times. To this day, it does not explicitly state that parents, sociocultural outfits or the police may not interfere in the sexual choices of adult offspring. It is left to children, if they have been assaulted or kidnapped, to approach the courts and accuse their own families or powerful militant groups with links to politicians. Some work up the courage, but in doing so, they court death.

India registered an 800 per cent increase in the number of 'honour' killings reported in recent years.[33] Police registered 288 cases between 2014 and 2016 alone, though activists suggest the numbers are higher. Most cases go unreported since it is usually families who report missing or dead children. With families doing the killing, who'd file a report? Officials also fail to document accurately, and some cases get passed off as accidental deaths.

It is hard to document how often cops collude with families to hunt down and forcibly separate couples. One of the ways they do this is by registering a case of rape against the man. Journalists analysed about 600 rape cases that were fully tried in just one city, Delhi, and learnt that 40 per cent turned out to be cases of consensual sex and elopement.[34]

Another way is to humiliate young people in public spaces. In 2005, in a town called Meerut, a bunch of police officers decided to devote themselves to public service in this manner. Local journalists were tipped off. Cameras were ready and rolling as the cops entered Meerut's Gandhi Park and began to round up people, chasing some, hitting others, forcing young men and women to raise their chins and face cameras. Television channels dutifully broadcast the footage.

Filmmaker Paromita Vohra tried to make sense of the assault through her film, *Morality TV aur Loving Jehad*. In one of her interviews, she said she was intrigued by the fact that 'stories about romancing young couples were reported by crime reporters, which was in itself curious – the location of love under crime'.

The Meerut assault had been codenamed Operation Majnu. Majnu – the name literally means 'crazy' – is the male protagonist of the legend of Laila-Majnu. Like Romeo, Majnu is a universally recognised tragic figure across the subcontinent. To call someone Romeo or Majnu was once a form of good-natured ribbing. Today, it is a threat.

The state of Uttar Pradesh assigned police personnel to 'Anti-Romeo' squads; other states promised to follow suit. Each squad was meant to include an officer of sub-inspector rank and four constables deployed in uniform as well as plainclothes. The director general of police of the time had reportedly tweeted: 'Safety of girls/ladies is the sole intent of the anti-Romeo squads. No moral policing.' But the state does not call them 'Women's Safety Squads'.

Writer and journalist Mrinal Pande describes such developments as a form of imperialism: 'Under the guise of upholding Indian traditions and protecting women, an anti-modern cultural imperialism is taking shape.'[35] Citizens are terrorised and the state refuses to reassure them.

I used to wonder why it mattered so much to politicians that people don't marry for love. Now I begin to see. Love is not a whipped-up sentiment, nor can it be whipped out of you. People cross borders, give up class and caste privilege for love. This is terrifying for politicians because it can make people re-examine identities.

Love is also the antidote to Partition. Therefore, a new language has been engineered wherein it is no compliment to be called Romeo. As for Juliet, she is not mentioned at all. Every so often we hear of a girl who risks her life for love. But young women are not referred to as Juliet or Laila by authority figures. By refusing to acknowledge them as lovers, the case can be made that women who fall in love are abducted or brainwashed, or forcibly converted.

It is a seamless continuation of the Partition rhetoric wherein each community had to prevent its girls being 'taken' while 'bringing' home girls of the other community. This trope plays out in popular culture too. Hindi films have often depicted interfaith couples on the run, willing to take on the world for love. But in most stories, the woman is Muslim. When cross-border love stories are written, the girl is Pakistani Muslim and the man – the 'hero' – is Hindu or Sikh.

Some films reverse the pattern. In one, *Kurban*, the Muslim man turns out to be part of a terrorist group. In another, *Anwar*, the Muslim boy is suspected of being a terrorist. *My Name is Khan* shows an autistic Muslim hero in the United States marrying a Hindu woman, a single mother. After 9/11, the child gets beaten to death by schoolyard bullies and the hero is banished from the woman's life until he can present his non-terrorist credentials to the American president.

There is one Partition drama, *Pinjar*, based on an iconic Punjabi novel. Its protagonist is a Hindu girl kidnapped by a Muslim man in revenge for the abduction of his aunt by her family. The book has the girl settling reluctantly into the marriage, having a baby and trying to raise an adopted baby of mixed or unknown blood. When she finally has an opportunity to return to her Hindu family, she chooses to stay back in Pakistan. The film obliterates the baby and the mixing of blood which had complicated the story of choice and what feels like home to the woman in the end.

One major Hindi film does show a mixed marriage in which the Muslim hero is neither terrorist nor gangster nor kidnapper.

It is a historical drama called *Jodha-Akbar*, based on Mughal emperor Akbar's relationship with his Hindu Rajput wife. It shows them coming to an understanding and their personal faiths not being disrupted by the alliance.

Theirs is not a unique marriage by any stretch. The founder of Azamgarh, Azam Khan, like most Muslim rulers in India, was only half Muslim. Mughal emperors, including Jehangir and Shah Jahan, were half or three-quarters of Hindu origin. The kings of the Deccan and of the south were also of mixed parentage. In fact, as Rima Hooja writes in *Rajasthan: A Concise History*, marriages between Muslim and Hindu Rajput rulers were not only common, the clans ensured at least five or six generations of intermarriage to cement the relationship.[36] Blood was not only mixed; the mixing was affirmed over and over.

Ordinary citizens also intermarried even up to the nineteenth century, when sustained campaigns were mounted against them. Around 1851–52, a clan of Bhatis decided to forbid such marriages, and the Sodha Rajputs of Jaisalmer were asked to stop giving daughters in marriage to Muslims, with threats of social ostracism.

Reformist Hindu groups also began to protest against interfaith unions, and once the rhetoric of Partition was in full swing, even kings could no longer take their own decisions. The ruler of Sirohi, Maharao Sir Sarup Ram Singh, had converted to Islam and married a Muslim woman but, in the 1940s, he was advised against declaring the fact openly, lest it trigger political unrest. He had no male heirs, and no descendants of mixed blood staked claim to his throne. Yet, when he died in 1946 and his will was found to contain instructions that he be buried with Muslim rites, there was a great flap. Some of his family and subjects, and Hindu organisations, lobbied hard to prevent the burial.[37] Had the ruler died in Sirohi instead of Delhi, it is possible even this – his last wish – would have been foiled.

The memory of the ruler's conversion has been buried as if it were a shameful secret. No histories honour his royal choice, nor mention the name of his Muslim wife along with other Hindu wives.

Mixed blood, which offered the possibility of love as well as a compelling tapestry of power, is a story that's been proactively erased from public memory. When *Jodha Akbar* was released, in 2008, multiple state governments imposed a ban upon film screenings.[38]

Politicians, news sources, movies, even researchers are careful to say nothing of couples who retain disparate religious identities or are able to find peace and happiness in new socio-spiritual identities. To admit that this is possible would be to admit that love is a fire that burns away your shell but does not necessarily hurt your core. It would certainly undo the lie of the two-nation theory.

*

Home, they say, is where the heart is. If home is a location of love, then in my country, home is a guilty secret. Or an apologetic, broken creature licking its wounds.

I cannot think of any city in India that is wholly safe for lovers. Having visited Bangladesh and Pakistan, I feel the same way about those countries. I cannot imagine walking with a man, arms linked, and not worrying about being questioned, humiliated, or worse.

The only place where I've seen people kiss each other in public is near the sea in Mumbai. Couples sit on the promenade or beach. They sit facing the grey-brown ocean, their backs turned to the city. When they think it is safe, they lock lips. The kisses rarely last more than a few seconds. I see girls kiss with one eye trained upon who is watching, measuring risk. The presence of other young people is, and is not, a measure of safety.

By and large, India's millennials tend to be wary of Romeo and bullying towards Juliet. A survey conducted by the Delhi-based Centre for the Study of Developing Societies and the Berlin-based Konrad Adenauer Stiftung says that nearly a quarter, 24 per cent, of Indians between the ages of 15 and

34 are extremely patriarchal in their outlook. Nearly half, girls included, disapproved of women wearing jeans. Every third woman disapproves of women working – that is, working outside the home and earning an independent income – after marriage; 53 per cent disapprove of dating and 45 per cent disapprove of interfaith marriages.

Perhaps it is fitting, then, that India should lay claim to being the final resting place of Laila and Majnu. There is no evidence that Laila and Majnu, whose name was Qais before he lost his sanity, ever existed. The story originated in Arabia and travelled overland to India. Legend has it that it wasn't just the story; the lovers themselves came to India.

In Rajasthan, on the India–Pakistan border, there is a tomb that houses two buried individuals. Some say, these are the lovers of legend, Laila and Majnu. Others say, it is the grave of a local Sufi saint and beside him, his favourite disciple. But regardless of who lies buried, people of all faiths are rumoured to visit. Perhaps they come hoping for a happier fate in love. Or perhaps, as the old Hindi film song goes, they weep and pray: let nobody ever fall in love; the cost is too steep.

Marital migration overwhelmingly affects women in India and their dislocation extends to the womb.

# 7 OUTSIDERS AT HOME

When they want to express displeasure about a daughter's behaviour, many Indian mothers are given to saying, *Is this how you'll behave when you go to your own home?* They don't mean a home she owns. Quite the opposite. They mean a husband's or in-laws' home where she will be an outsider and each gesture, each meal could turn into an indictment of her upbringing.

My mother never asked much of me by way of chores. She didn't discriminate between me and my brother, but when she wanted to pull me in line, she too was liable to say, *Is this how you'll behave when . . .*

She assumed it was just a matter of time. Someday, I'd live with in-laws and would have to be on my best behaviour, twenty-four-seven. It was, and is, the done thing. The census of 2011 shows that 'marriage' is the single biggest cause of internal migration in India and, in this category of migrant, women comprise 98.4 per cent. There remain strong taboos against men who move in with wives' families, and the *ghar jamai*, resident son-in-law, is often an object of ridicule.

There are old sayings in Hindi that raising a daughter is like tilling someone else's field, that she is *parāya dhan*, an asset that belongs to someone else. You couldn't afford to grow too attached, for she would not stay. So, while you hoped the husband's home would become a true home for her, you schooled her to act like she belonged marginally, constantly appeasing the owners of *that* home.

Most marriages in India continue to be arranged, which means the couple is not in love when the woman moves in.

Surveys from 2018 show that, even in urban areas, over 90 per cent of people in their twenties have had arranged marriages.[1] What this means is that women must learn to live with strangers.

We have always understood that living with in-laws is fraught. Folk songs and literature are strewn with metaphors and images of the *maika, pīhar, naihar* or *bābul kā ghar*. A father's home, a maternal homestead. The metaphor has been extended to mean homeland by poets such as the exiled ruler of Avadh, Wajid Ali Shah. His popular nineteenth-century composition 'Babul Mora Naihar Chhooto Jaaye' (Father, my home is slipping away) is written in the voice of a bride for whom the threshold of her childhood home is now transformed into a foreign land.

The metaphor has also been extended to the spiritual-temporal schism. A popular song from the Hindi cinema of the 1960s spells it out rather directly: 'Vo duniya mere bābul ka ghar; ye duniya sasurāl', 'The other world is my father's home; this world is my in-laws' house'.[2] The natal home was thus the true one, the one you ached for.

A distinct genre of songs of *bidāi*, leave-taking, was written for both: the bride and those who must let her go. They never fail to move me for they are pleadings on the part of the girl not to be sent away, or blessings that the girl is so well loved in the new home that she forgets her own family.

There was a finality to this leave-taking, and to underline the cleave, a woman's natal family would rarely visit. In many north Indian families, fathers would say that they did not even drink water in their daughters' home. It was a symbolic double lock on a shut door. A woman could visit her parents, at leisure and with her husband's permission, but she must not think she could return at will. Additionally, she couldn't presume that her parents were welcome in *that* home; her in-laws must have no excuse to resent her on the grounds that her family cost them the slightest bit of trouble.

In the global west, too, a sense of grief accompanies traditional weddings. Fathers 'give away' brides, and their loss is real. An unmarried daughter could be counted upon for her labour, her time, her affection, and could be chastised. A married daughter was off bounds.

A wedding may be joyful, but marriage was also financial cleavage. A girl was showered with gifts, assets apart from jewellery and money. To secure her happiness, even her safety in an alien environment, the in-laws were showered with gifts too. This was done even by families that could ill afford it, and many fathers courted ruin by taking hefty loans or mortgaging land to pay dowries.

Families were also under pressure to let go of prepubescent girls. Naturally, little girls would not control their own wealth, nor would money and gifts be returned very easily if they were widowed or deserted.

Until the nineteenth and early twentieth centuries, to be free of a husband was to risk homelessness. Divorce or annulment was not permissible for Hindus. Widows were not always welcome in their fathers' homes. Many Hindu widows committed – or were made to commit – sati, where they were burnt alive along with dead husbands. A total of 8,134 cases were recorded just between 1815 and 1828, before sati was outlawed in 1829.

Strict rules were formulated for widows while they lived. Eating simple meals, without spices and even without salt, frequent fasts, or eating only one meal a day, wearing only one colour, no jewellery, no make-up, no hairdos. Sometimes their heads were shaved. Many widows were sent away to pilgrimage sites like Mathura and Banaras,[3] where they sang hymns and chanted and hoped for the bare minimum:[4] a place to sleep, a roof, a bit of bread.

Inheritance rules changed with the Hindu Succession Act of 1956. Women could now will property as they liked, but it was only in 2005 that the Indian laws were amended to let daughters inherit an equal share.

Muslims have their own Personal Law, which does ensure inheritance, albeit not an equal share for daughters. However, even this unequal share is not always given despite it being a Quranic obligation. Part of the reason inheritance is difficult to secure is marital dislocation. How do you tell your brothers that you want them to give up the land they've worked, or that you want them to sell half of the house in which they live?

What families offer instead is a dowry. Trouble is, dowries are not home. Money can buy a woman a room she legally owns, but it can't buy social support or safety.

If a husband was abusive or demanded money, every effort was made to dissuade a daughter from returning to her parents. I have heard of more than one acquaintance – upper-class women of my own generation – whose parents sent them back to their husbands and in-laws despite complaints of abuse.

In the old days, brides – especially upper-caste women whose mobility was limited – were told by mothers and grandmothers to remember that once the *doli* (a palanquin in which brides were carried away) was set down in the husband's home, they must try to leave only on the *arthi*, the funeral bier. It was part advice to make the marriage work, part warning not to come running back if they were in trouble. And trouble there most certainly was.

Dowries turned into a form of extortion and torture, and that special category of South Asian homicide: dowry death. So frequent was the phenomenon of 'bride burning' – young wives being set on fire so the crime could be explained as a kitchen accident – that in addition to existing anti-dowry laws, in 1983, new laws were enacted to allow the police to arrest a husband or his family members as soon as a wife complained of harassment. It did give some pause to the violence and its methodology, but it hasn't prevented murder.

In 2011, I was at a courthouse in a small town in central India where I met a man fighting to get his daughter's killers punished. His lawyer, a woman, kept referring to a *hādsā*, an accident or incident, and for several minutes I didn't even realise that the daughter was already dead and that this was not a compensation suit but a homicide.

I had to bite down gall to keep talking to that father. His daughter told him about the demands, the threats. But he didn't take her away from her husband's home. He didn't even tell his daughter to leave and file a police complaint about harassment. Who knows what he told her? To hang in there?

He kept saying that he had already forked over a large dowry, of his own volition. When I asked why, he stared, as if it had never struck him that he should not have. As if all fathers don't know the risks of sending a girl into a hostile and greedy environment.

Listening to my arguments, his lawyer had sniffed and said, it's a social evil. Society would have to change. It hasn't changed. In 2017, offences registered under the Dowry Prohibition Act numbered 10,189; dowry deaths numbered 7,466. These are just the ones reported. Most families do not report until there's actual violence or if wives are thrown out, or threatened, or until women's fathers meet their demands.

Most people do not want to deal with such fears and pressures. So, they start to dislodge daughters as quickly as possible. It begins with being ejected from the first home we all have – the womb – and then the second one, the nourishment of our infancy. Female infanticide and foeticide have been persistent trends in India, where the sex ratio is 919 female infants to every 1,000 males. Sex determination tests are rampant. Sex selective abortions are an illegal industry.[5]

If they survive, daughters are breastfed less than sons, and the disparity increases as they grow.[6] They get less protein.[7] Women are more often vegetarian[8] and not always of their own volition. Female students in institutions like the Banaras Hindu University have complained that they are not served meat at all in their hostels.[9]

The emphasis on being thin, diminutive, compliant, sweet natured – somehow *manageable* – is well documented all over the world, with the possible exception of matriarchal and matrilineal societies.

I myself do not remember when and how I picked up the notion that 'boys eat more', that this was a scientific fact, and in accordance with justice. The assumption was, sons needed to eat more because they were out more, doing physical labour. They worked the land, ran errands, or went rowing and horse-riding. Besides, overfed men were excused: a paunch was seen as an attractive sign of prosperity.

Despite being the daughter of a very active mother who worked very long hours, it took many years for me to wonder whether feminine labours were less physical, and what justice there was in daughters *not* working the land, or just riding out for pleasure.

The roots of feminine dislocation run thousands of years deep, extending not only to assets but to our bodies. The ancient Indian text, *Artha Shastra*, estimated to have been written in around 150 CE, describes how women's movements were to be curtailed, as long as the women were not courtesans, in which case they were encouraged to travel even with battle expeditions.[10] A wife had to take permission from her husband to 'go on pleasure trips and could not leave the house when he was drunk or asleep'. If women committed adultery, punishments included nose and ear being cut off.

Slavery, too, existed, and one route to freedom was for a female slave to give birth to a child fathered by her master. But if a non-slave woman had sex with a male slave, that is, a man of her own choosing, her punishment was death.

There was little difference between a wife and a slave in the sense that both were uprooted, physically and psychologically. A woman's sexual choice was easily overridden. She didn't control the fruits of her labour and, just like slaves, couldn't leave. It was not for nothing that wives in many cultures referred to husbands as lord and master.

That men continue to think of themselves as masters of women's bodies is evidenced by a global trail of blood; 58 per cent of female homicides globally are women killed by partners, in-laws, or their own families.[11]

Many women are also internally dislocated, distanced from their well-being to the extent that damage to, or humiliation of, their own bodies appears acceptable. In India, the National Family Health Survey released in 2016 said that 52 per cent of women believe it was okay for husbands to beat wives, and at least 31 per cent of married women experienced physical, sexual, or emotional violence by their husbands.

Cases of 'cruelty by husband and his relatives' are reported as a distinct category of crime, and 110,000 cases were reported in 2016. This is barely a fraction of the hundreds of millions who admit to actually suffering cruelty. They do not report either because they have ceased to think of damage to themselves as cruelty, or because they have nowhere else to go. It is hard to live in the marital home, with in-laws, after all, if a woman gets her husband arrested. An awareness of how police and judicial systems work – the time, the expense! – does not help.

For unmarried women too, most perpetrators of sexual violence are relatives (27 per cent).[12] If a woman reports her own family, where does she go?

The alternative is the capital 'H' Home: a shelter where she must live among strangers, subject to the will of the state. If she is able to leave and find a personal shelter, however ramshackle, she is afraid of assault by outsiders who see that she no longer has the protection of her kin.

In many Indian cities, single women are not welcome. I have had trouble renting homes myself, although I did have the support of my family. The bodies of unattached women – not so different, after all, from the 'unguarded' woman of the ancient texts – are seen as sites of trouble: men are likely to take an interest, regardless of their own marital status, and all interest is monitored. As unattached individuals, women are seen as unworthy of independent living.

If home is a place of safety, where, then, is home for women? Privately, most women accept that it is not a place of absolute safety, nor a place where they can be who they are. It is a roof, meals and, with any luck, some piece of your heart. The true home is elsewhere.

*

My mother didn't consciously pass on to me the expectation of feminine dislodging. It just slipped in through the cultural cracks.

Part of me acknowledges, Mom was not wrong in her assumptions. In *that* house, I would likely be subject to harsher scrutiny. Husband, mother-in-law, even sisters-in-law could tell me what to wear, where to go or not go, at what time. Earning their disapproval would make my position at home more tenuous.

A girl has to be prepared to surrender freedom, custom, politics. Friends and cousins parroted these assumptions: *A girl has to be adjustable.* Pliancy was a virtue. Obstinacy was a failing. Homely was a virtue. Unrestricted mobility – going where you wanted, with or without permission – was inconceivable.

The Indian Human Development Survey released in 2016 found that 74 per cent of Indian women need permission from parents, husbands or in-laws to step out of the house, even if it was just to see a doctor; 58 per cent need permission to go to the grocery store. Although 27 per cent of women had paid jobs, only 5 per cent felt they had any real control over who they would get married to.

That I grew into womanhood with a feeling of dispossession that I could not articulate is not surprising after all. My body, my city, even my culture was not my own to inhabit. Obstinate and argumentative, I was the opposite of most feminine virtues advertised in the matrimonial columns of the newspapers. Worse, I was afraid that I might actually be persuaded, seduced, scolded into inhabiting those virtues and surrendering my selfhood.

In major and minor ways, women are prepped to 'move' against instinct. A wife's personal appearance and behaviour is the depository of both, the culture she marries into *and* the culture she inherits. In migrant communities, there is greater pressure on women to carry the baggage of 'home' on their bodies. This could mean covered heads or veils while men have wholesale abandoned traditional attire, or colleges forbidding jeans for female students. It is understood that men adapt to be accepted into better paying jobs. For women, it is understood that they will struggle against their own convenience.

Besides, the assumption that, through marriage, a woman surrenders her whole self puts her citizenship, and that of her children, in jeopardy. In Nepal, a debate has raged about discriminatory laws that do not grant citizenship through maternal descent. If a woman marries a foreign national, her children may not be acknowledged as citizens.[13]

In India, there is a worse problem, with married women themselves being at risk of disenfranchisement and detention as 'foreigners'. The National Registry of Citizens drawn up in Assam left out 2.9 million women because they 'failed to establish blood links with their paternal families'.[14] They no longer had documentary proof of being 'from' their fathers' home address.

*

My mother has seen me find my feet in new cities, pay rent, even cook. She's stopped asking me to fall in line, lest I move into a less forgiving household. Sometimes, though, hesitantly and wistfully, she talks of me leaving. Not leaving her home; leaving *her*. Who knows if I'll be welcome, she says, in *that* home?

I can tell her that she will be welcome in *my* home. But how can I guarantee her welcome in a home in which I am uncertain of my own place?

I am among the lucky 5 per cent of women in my country who can choose who to marry. For my generation of financially independent women, some of the biggest emotional negotiations are about place: the right to live on our own, to live with neither parents nor partners, to discuss with potential partners whether we can move into a neutral place rather than with *his* family? And can our old parents also live with us?

The paradox is that those of us who can negotiate our place are rarely called 'homely', no matter how many homes we make.

A divisive political rhetoric ensures that even a final resting place becomes contested ground.

# 8 GRAVE POLITICS

The first burial I ever saw was in my grandmother's garden in Lucknow. I was a small child, upset at the destruction of a plastic parrot. Because it was shaped like a living creature, I felt it had 'died'. Death requires solemn ritual, so my brother and cousins buried the broken 'bird'.

Grandma had an affinity for soil. Despite the limitations of a city garden, she grew papayas, ladies' fingers, lemons, herbs, flowers. She also had a keen sense of her own end. In preparation, she had bought herself a *kafan* (shroud), set aside money for her burial and let her family know, so nobody could say that she owed anyone anything after she was gone.

I don't worry much about funeral expenses. Perhaps this is because I have been financially independent long enough not to care about proving it beyond the grave. Still, I inherited from Grandma a certain preoccupation with burial. I wrote one novella set in a graveyard. I gravitate towards Urdu couplets that use burials, funereal baths and biers as metaphor. I visit tombs, cenotaphs, necropolises, pausing to read names and epitaphs. Dutch, Armenian, English, Scottish, French: wherever they came from, here they rest.

When we last visited one of our ancestral villages, Karhan, one of my mother's cousins pointed out the spot where my great-grandfather lies buried, and said, 'You all should put up a stone with his name on it. Our generation is the last one that remembers who is buried where.'

I felt myself bristle, then heard myself declare that I would pay for the stone and the engraving if nobody else would. It was a curious reaction. I had been arguing at the time with my mother, telling her not to waste money on building inside our ancestral house. We visited so rarely, what was the point? Yet there I was, offering to spend money on a gravestone. Is this what they call, 'the call of blood'?

*

Home is where others come looking for you, in life and after. Those who come looking are most often your own blood, but sometimes you also return to those with whom you have a spiritual bond. Sometimes, it is the returning that cements the bond.

Among Shias, the burial sites of Hazrat Ali, his son Hussain and other Imams are treated as sites of pilgrimage. But most do not go that far. They go to the nearest *imambara*, which houses symbolic replicas and is where ritual mourning is enacted year upon year. In returning to their native place, families also return to small imambaras in the village, and even within the walls of the household.

My mother returned to the village in staccato. In Moharram, she sews a velvet *chādar*, or coverlet, edged with silver or gold lace, for the tomb of a Sufi called Mir Shamsi in Karhan. Our family draws its lineage from him.

In Sufi thought, death is a sort of homecoming. A verse attributed to al-Ghazali compares the body to a cage and the spirit to a bird that has flown: 'I praise God who hath set me free / and made for me a dwelling in the heavenly heights'.[1] In the Indian subcontinent, Madho Lal Hussein wrote: 'Come home, the grave calls you.'[2] The death anniversary of Sufis is celebrated rather than birth because, as Rumi said: 'The grave is a curtain hiding the communion of paradise.' Their graves, and sites where relics are preserved, get visitors from all communities, and offerings include flowers, incense and decorative chādars. The saints are remembered as much for their attitude to power – many lived in poverty and rejected an exclusionary orthodoxy – as for their spiritual practice. Some visitors come hoping for divine intercession via those who were assumed to have access to God. Some seek cures and amulets. Many come merely to visit, as you would go to an elder or a teacher.

Even when graves are not linked with saints, they are reminders of the next world, and are therefore treated with respect. Any violation is experienced as an insult, and is often intended as such. Whenever graves associated with a minority are targeted, it is that community's right to live that is under attack. In India, in 2002, during the anti-Muslim violence in Gujarat, the tomb of Wali Dakhani was destroyed.[3] He was not a saint but a poet who had written high praise about the state of Gujarat. The violence ended but no attempt was made to restore the grave. A road was built over it. There was nothing left by way of memorial – not a plaque, not a note of regret.

Travelling through Gujarat in 2006, I had noticed the cab driver's reluctance to drive me to cemeteries. He could not distinguish between Dutch and English cemeteries and Muslim ones. The word he used for all was *makkarba* (*maqbara* or 'tomb'), and when I persisted, he told me to go ask Muslim shopkeepers because 'Ye Miya log ki jagah Miya hi jaante hain', 'Only Muslims know about Muslim places'. In his eyes, a cemetery was not a reminder of the other place, where all of us eventually go, but *the other's* place. Therefore, unworthy of visitation.

Mundane, everyday symbols of Muslim lives – food, clothing, prayers – have been targeted before, but in recent years, there is a hostile focus on graveyards. A singer of Bhojpuri songs shot into the national headlines spouting lyrics like 'Jo na bole Jai Shree Ram / Usko Bhejo Kabristan', 'Those who don't hail Lord Ram must be sent to the graveyard'.[4] It was an obvious incitement to violence and the singer was booked. However, politicians, too, have been dividing people via burial sites.

Prime Minister Modi himself campaigned in Uttar Pradesh saying, 'If you create a *kabristaan* (graveyard) in a village, then a *shamshaan* (cremation ground) should also be created.'[5] The current chief minister of Uttar Pradesh, Yogi Adityanath, asked voters to send rival parties to the *kabristān*, a word picked out carefully to suggest that his rivals were allied with minorities, from whom he was distancing himself.[6] In fact, he specifically warned that if his party was not elected, state resources would be used up to create mosques and graveyards.[7]

Graves are not Muslim. Nor Christian, nor Jewish. Nor is cremation Hindu. Pagan religions typically had both cremation and burial traditions. A grave was merely proof of life, a record of existence and loss. Among the oldest surviving human arte-facts in India are megaliths and dolmens, indicating burial.[8] Cairns, or rock burials, have been found.[9]

Ancient Harappans and Aryans were familiar with burials. The Rig Veda, composed between 1700 BCE and 1100 BCE, refers to a *kurgan*, a roofed burial chamber supported by posts, and horse sacrifices were part of royal funerals.[10] There is men-tion of both cremation and burial, with verses emphasising 'the softness and gentleness of the welcoming earth, both mother and bride, which lies lightly on the dead man'.

Over time, cremation became the norm for caste Hindus, but India's remarkable heterodoxy means a great variety of death rites. Dalits, outside the caste hierarchy, often bury the dead. In *Death in Banaras*, Jonathan Parry has described other categories of burials within the Hindu fold: children, lepers, the childless, and ascetics who are considered to have left the material world while still alive.[11]

In Kolkata, there are at least three Hindu graveyards, and reporters have noted that people leave objects like cloth, candles, slippers, even medicine, while some children are buried with things they liked to eat.[12] A burial ground in Bengaluru has tomb-stones and epitaphs with sculptures of the sacred Nandi bull and lings to denote the worship of Lord Shiva.[13] The Lingayat commu-nity buries the dead in a sitting position.[14] Other south Indian communities that bury the dead include the Vokkaligas, Kurubas, Reddys, Pisharody, certain Gond clans, the Kodavas.[15]

In Mumbai, there's a graveyard in the heart of town that belongs to the Dashnami Goswami community, a monastic group that buries the dead after rubbing the body down with ash, dressing it in saffron robes, a *rudraksh* (prayer bead seed) necklace and a bag to represent ascetic antecedents. The Sahi were another Hindu group that buried the dead recumbent while the Vani buried in the seated, *padmasana* position.[16] Followers of the Pranami faith also buried the dead.[17] In Rajasthan, burials were documented[18] among the Kalbeliya Mewara, Tonwar Rajput, Kaamad of the Alakh panth, Meghwals who follow Guru Ramdeo-ji, the Siddh who follow Jasnath-ji, the Khaaradia Sirvis, followers of the saint Aiji,[19] and the Kathodi.[20]

The Garāsiya community I spoke with in Sirohi also confirmed that while ordinary tribesmen are cremated, never the Bhopa or priest. He is always buried. Another ascetic group, the Nath Jogis were traditionally buried. The Jogis could identify as Hindu or Muslim, or neither.[21] Yogi Adityanath, who belongs to this order, should know better than to complain about graveyards.

Perhaps he does know better. However, most people don't. Growing up with a singular narrative of Hinduism, I too had internalised the burial–cremation binary. There was nothing in my education, in literature or popular culture that smashed this false binary. Every Hindu character that died on screen was cremated. Children were rarely shown being buried or immersed in rivers, as is the actual practice. The only visible and remarked-upon Hindu burials were those of political leaders who consciously rejected upper-caste practices, as some did in south India.

Dalits form over 16 per cent of India's population and have traditionally been required to perform labours that nobody else would – handling sewage, animal and human waste, corpses – and were often forced to live on the fringes of the village; the community has limited access to the performance of death rites. There are reports of Dalits being turned away from crematoria, or having to perform rites at home.[22] Access to a crematorium can be blocked, and videos have surfaced of Dalits having to airdrop a body from a bridge to ground level to avoid the 'upper caste area'.[23]

Discrimination does not end with death, nor with religious conversion. In Christian graveyards, too, especially where the land is owned by individuals, there is evidence of segregation: Dalits buried on one side of a wall, upper-caste converts on the other side.[24] Activists identifying as Pasmanda or lower-caste Muslims have also flagged the issue of denial of burial rights on lands controlled by the Muslim elite.[25]

Dalits and Muslims also complain of graveyards being taken over for other purposes. Not all graveyards are public land. Most are private properties declared *wakf*, that is, land or buildings donated by Muslims for the welfare of the community and managed by a board. In Delhi, a 1970 document noted the existence of 488 Muslim graveyards, and yet, only twenty-five to thirty of these could be used for their intended purpose.[26]

Attempts to take over burial lands have led to lawsuits, fights, even murder. Journalist Saeed Naqvi mentions covering a 'riot' in Gopalgarh, Rajasthan, where police entered a mosque and shot dead six Muslims in 2011. At the heart of the violence was a set of three properties – a mosque, a two-acre enclosure for special Eid prayers, and a graveyard that had been encroached.[27]

*

When someone dies, Muslims are taught to say *Inna ilahi wa inna ilahi rajioon*. From God we come and to God we return. Parry writes that informed Hindu priests also describe a hierarchy of liberation: *salokya* (residence in the same world of God), *samipya* (living in proximity to God), *sarupya* (acquiring the form of God) and, the highest, *sayujya* (complete union with God 'as water mixes with water').[28] This is not very different from Sufi or Christian ideas of the soul's return to God, who is the ultimate home.

I know neither Arabic nor Sanskrit, but sometimes I develop a feeling for earth like marrow in my bones. I feel an attachment for the Hindi word: *mitti*. Soil. The shell, garment, cage of the body is dust. Or ash. Those who cremate also need rituals connected with nature – water, if not land. Ashes are floated in rivers. Some people ask for ashes to be scattered in a place where they felt most alive. The soul may or may not be liberated, but we all want to return to the elements in some tangible form. Some of us actively seek out the elements when we want to exit this world.

A boatman in Banaras once told me that he was afraid I was going to kill myself. I was on assignment in a city that draws millions of tourists and is renowned for its silk trade, but where weavers were starving. In the evening, I'd hired a boat on the Ganga. The boatman was a nervous greying figure, perhaps wondering if he was morally bound to try and rescue me. It was only after I took an oar and demanded that he teach me to row that he was persuaded, I wasn't seeking a watery grave.

What made him think such a thing? He shrugged. People come here to die, he said. That I insisted on being his sole passenger, and was dressed in a white saree that made me look like a young Hindu widow, didn't help.

Very few drown themselves, but it is true that people come here to die. Banaras, also called Varanasi or Kashi, has been seen as a place of salvation for as long as anyone can remember. Ancient Sanskrit texts proclaimed: 'Those whose bones, hair, nails, and flesh fall in Kashi will reside in heaven even though they be great sinners.' Funeral pyres burn day and night on the banks of the river. Millions come, hoping for *mukti*, liberation. But, as Jonathan Parry writes, 'The problem starts as soon as one enquires what death in Kashi is a liberation *from*.'[29]

The range of responses to this question is extremely wide. The commonest is that it is a 'cessation of coming and going' – that is, the end of rebirth. The popular view of what liberation means was that it is 'a perpetual and sybaritic residence in heaven'. One of Parry's informants described it as a place where a *rasgulla* (sweet) would be magically conjured if you wanted one. Another described it as the antithesis of *this* world. Heaven, then, is an idealised homeland: a place of fulfilment, where you never feel thwarted, where evil is barred. A safe place.

Hell is the opposite, a slightly exaggerated version of the evils that befall us. A place where tortures never cease, and full of others like ourselves.

*

I once read an obituary of a homeless man, a rickshaw puller called Mohammed Abdul Kasim Ali Shaikh, who had lived briefly in a shelter in Delhi.[30]

This brief shelter brought him in contact with activists; that's how there was an article telling us about his life – that he was a survivor of childhood abuse, was HIV positive, was not bitter but friendly, that he worked for his daily bread till the day he died, that he was killed in an accident while he slept on the road divider. The writer, Harsh Mander, posed a question: 'Homeless and destitute. Leaving no trace behind him that he had ever lived. Was his life and death indeed of no consequence?'

The question stopped me. Leaving no trace, are our lives of consequence? The question can be tweaked: if we are not allowed to leave some trace of our existence, are we being informed that we are inconsequential?

Graves of prominent men and soldiers' memorials are sites of public memory and are maintained as such to assert consequence. Governments, armies, city and village councils determine who has a right to be remembered. Groups with less power are denied memorial space, and thereby, their claims upon the land are further weakened.

In an article about the discovery of a mass grave in New York in 1991, Edward Rothstein wrote that cemeteries are the locus of tribute and memory, affirming connections to a place. Old maps had confirmed the existence of a 'Negro Burial Ground' and this transformed New York's understanding of its history. 'Among the scars left by the heritage of slavery, one of the greatest is an absence: where are the memorials, cemeteries, architectural structures or sturdy sanctuaries that typically provide the ground for a people's memory?'[31]

Disadvantaged groups, like Dalits and Adivasis in India, have fewer visible memorials with which they might identify. Statues of Dalit icons like Dr Ambedkar, who led the team drafting the Constitution of India, have been defaced. The commemoration of an 1818 battle in which Dalit soldiers of the

Mahar regiment routed the Maratha forces led by Brahmin Peshwas, has become contentious again in recent years. A board marking the grave of a Mahar (Dalit) leader was damaged in 2017, and then went missing, which led to tensions and clashes with other groups.

Many striking monuments in India relate to mausoleums of Muslim rulers and nobles, including the Taj Mahal in Agra. The Supreme Court has already remarked on state neglect causing the latter's deterioration, while Hindu groups have been trying to make the case that it used to be a temple, and have conducted Hindu rituals in its vicinity.[32] In Maharashtra, there have been attempts to destroy the tomb of a Muslim soldier who was killed whilst trying to kill Shivaji, a seventeenth-century king who has been appropriated as a mascot of Hindutva groups.[33]

An octogenarian writer, Govind Pansare, who tried to bring historical context to local politics by writing a book called *Shivaji Kon Hota?* (*Who Was Shivaji?*), detailing the ruler's life and his largely secular and diverse administration, was assassinated in 2015. The state has not honoured his memory or his work through any memorials.

*

There is a poet called Rahat Indori, from the city of Indore. Urdu poets have often taken on noms de plume with a city name as a suffix. Nearly every town in the Hindi-speaking belt can boast its own poet, whether in residence or in exile. For instance, Daag Dehlavi of Delhi, Kaifi Azmi of Azamgarh, Shamim Karhani of Karhan.

One of Rahat Indori's couplets is often quoted, and when he recites it at public events, he never fails to draw cries of approval and applause:

> *Sabhi ka khoon hai shaamil yahaan ki mitti mein*
> *Kisi ke baap ka Hindustan thodi hai!*

> Everybody's blood is mixed into the earth here,
> Hindustan does not belong to anybody's father!

The verse has the ring of a double truth: people of all races and faiths have given their blood to the land. Like it or not, anybody who is buried here, belongs here. It fills me with sadness, though, to hear the other truth: the couplet is a riposte to people who imply that some of us do not belong in this land, that some people are indeed acting as if the country was their personal property.

When I begin to despair, I think of Chaman/Rizwan. The newspaper had carried a story about a 'mentally challenged' youth who succeeded in uniting two communities.[34] The boy was born into a Hindu household, but wandered off and got lost before he was adopted by a Muslim family. His mother found him and brought him back, but he kept disappearing, going back to his other family. When he died, the families initially squabbled about whether his body should be burnt or buried. Finally, a golden balance was achieved: he was buried, like a child, in the Hindu cremation ground, with priests reading verses from both the Quran and the Gita.

Sometimes, I tell myself, Hindustan is where anything is possible. Kabir was possible only in Kashi, after all.

Weaver-saint-poet Kabir, born into or adopted by a Muslim family, devoted himself to a Hindu guru who would not embrace him. He was eventually acknowledged as a spiritual force who distanced himself from all orthodoxies. True, he was pressured into leaving Kashi. Towards the end of his life, he went to Magahar, a place where priests said salvation was impossible. It is also said that when he died, there was a squabble about last rites – burial or cremation? The matter was resolved through a miracle. Lifting the shroud, his followers found not a body but a bunch of flowers. People were free to divide these remnants and perform any ritual they chose.

That Kabir, and his poetry, survived and that his fame only grew in the centuries after his death is another miracle. Kashi, the city that disowned him, is forever linked with his name, and even though we do not know if he was buried, there is a 'tomb' – or shrine, if you prefer – that we can visit by way of remembrance.[35]

*

What is this need to put name on mud? But I *am* tempted. I want an epitaph. Perhaps it is the same feeling that made me scratch my name on the rocks of the hills of my childhood. An epitaph, like a name-plate on the door of a rented apartment. Some words to stave off fears of amnesia and isolation. While we sleep the eternal sleep, suppose someone should miss us, they should know where to come find us.

They say all children long to be seen. Don't all grown-ups long for it too: to be seen, to not be forgotten the moment your back is turned? Is choosing to go into the earth and writing your name on a stone also not a way of sending down roots?

Sometimes I wonder if I should set aside money for the purpose. My poor grandmother probably didn't know that it isn't just shrouds and funerals that cost money. Finding a spot in a graveyard costs money these days. Besides, there is the question of where: which corner of the world would I choose, if I could choose?

In India, we make a distinction between *janm-bhoomi*, birthplace, and *karm-bhoomi*, a place of work or purpose. Mumbai has been my karm-bhoomi. So have other cities, for one must go wherever one finds bread. However, whenever I find myself in the grip of anxiety or sadness, I shut my eyes and try to conjure a place of safety, a place where I can go as I am. What I see is a cluster of graves.

The memory of my maternal grandparents intercedes in my struggle to find a way to belong somewhere. Grandma rarely expressed any material desires, but she did say that she wanted to be buried next to her husband. She died in another city but, in keeping with her wishes, we brought her body to Lucknow and buried her near my grandfather. A great-grandmother, other great-aunts and uncles are also buried in the vicinity. I visit those graves, touch the grass that sprouts atop, and mourn afresh their loss, the ideals they tried to live up to. When I cannot visit, I think of them, and make plans to visit whenever I can.

There is no longer any adolescent drama, but I did buy a tiny bit of land to call my own. Not my mother's, not my father's. Mine. When it came to deciding where, I chose Lucknow. The city is tied up with the happier memories of my childhood. It may change yet – people, accents, the names of parks or markets, its particular cosmopolitanism may be lost. But there's this: at least two people who loved me without condition lie buried here.

Questions of belonging trouble me very little now. When people ask where home is, I now have an answer.

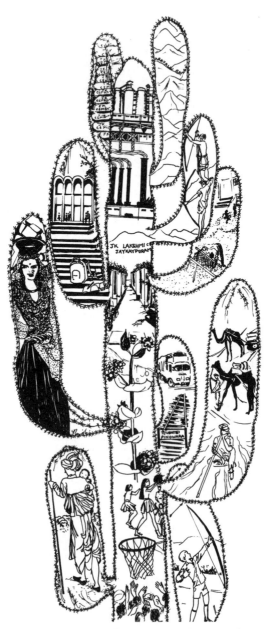

Belonging is a shifting portrait of memory, sentiment and compulsion.

# 9  PLACE LIKE HOME

Hindi poet Agyega wrote a long poem called 'Ghar'[1] in which he struggles with home as a mysterious, slippery concept:

> Everyone keeps to themselves
> Home talk
> Nobody tells another
> What we talk of
> Is not home[2]

Home is unspeakably personal. As Agyeya's play of words suggests, it can be unpleasant or embarrassing, like a family secret. Most people will not reveal their true experience of home if you asked them to describe it.

I, for instance, have felt at home in India despite its hunger, its crushing shortages of transport and healthcare services. I might be irritated at certain behaviours, such as people's tendency to occupy a counter in a cluster rather than lining up at a respectful distance. Lines described as 'snaking' are less like a singular snake and more like a hydra. Women demand, and get, separate queues not on account of chivalry but because it is unbearable having male strangers breathing – very literally – down our necks. Still, I've learnt how to request distance, in what tone of voice, when to stick out an elbow, and when to hit a man.

If I want to take a bathroom break – or even a lunch break – while keeping my place in a queue, I know how to do it. The cluster-queue does not think that 'order' is in itself valuable. What is more valuable is trust, however fleeting, in one's neighbours. You should be able to tell people: this is my place, guard it for me. And when you return, the person behind you will return your spot to you.

Here, I know the nuances of social behaviour. I know how to rearrange a relationship by switching between just three words – *aap*, *tum* and *tu* – all of which mean the same thing: 'you'. They are used variably depending on whether love is intended or annoyance, familiarity or disrespect. *Tu*, for instance, is almost never used in my family. It is too familiar, too likely to be misinterpreted as an insult. And yet, people often use *tu* for God. Here, I know when love and respect ceases to interfere with intimacy.

On longer train journeys, strangers have plonked their babies in my lap, or squeezed themselves tighter to make room for me when I did not have a reserved seat or berth. The dangerously overcrowded local trains in Mumbai have their own unwritten rules. Women have devised a 'claim' system although no formal reservation is allowed. You ask a seated passenger where she's getting off, and if nobody else has 'claimed' the seat, you ask her to 'give it' to you when she leaves. The system works because everyone accepts that it is the only way 'first come, first served' can be implemented under adverse circumstances, that whoever has been standing longer deserves to sit down for a while. Like a family secret, I inhabit these systems, even defend them when they're under fire from non-familiar people.

To ask whether there's still no place like home implies that, for many people, home could be no place or, equally, every place. For people who are able to travel in relative safety and can return from the other end of the world within a day, it is potentially 'every place'. However, to say 'There's no place like home' is to refer to a place where our right to be is not in question. We may suffer here, but it is important that we are not singled out for suffering. Home is where suffering is shared out, like bread, and or a three-seat bench shared by four.

*

In his poem about home, Agyeya wrote:

> I am my own home
> Nobody lives at home
> Do even I live in my home?

The body is habitation. It is the first, principal and final home of all organisms. In the crumbling of the body, in our desire to survive – at least as a memory – we are the same. Everywhere we go, we strive to belong with others, but also to our own selves. A state of dispossession often assails women and children who cannot control how their bodies are treated, and men too, whenever they confront similarly hostile conditions.

Extreme poverty and its corollary, great wealth, also determine the contours of home. Extremely vulnerable individuals belong precariously even in their own bodies.

In India, the official poverty line is a per capita income of 32 rupees per day for rural and 47 rupees for urban residents. I had once toyed with the idea of putting myself on a 47-rupee daily budget in Mumbai. I wasn't accounting for rent but I started to document living expenses, with the assumption that I had a job that would bring me these poverty wages.

Travelling into town and back cost more than 47 rupees, even if I took only buses and trains. I considered walking everywhere but I was a woman in public space and, even in a relatively safe city, there were comments, propositions. I found myself looking for other women so I could hang about in their midst, hoping to be spared humiliation. I hadn't even begun to eat.

For a week, I totted up my grocery bills – rice, lentils, vegetables, milk, sugar – not buying anything except basics. Then I gave up the exercise. Making the list was triggering anxiety and I dared not push myself further. I did learn one crucial thing, though: if I was actually at or below the poverty line, especially if I had children to feed, all the things that lend me a feeling of home – language, history, memory – would dissolve into the overwhelming consideration of hunger. Food would be home.

Home is malleable, then. Firstly in the sense that an existing location may end up being adversarial to one's well-being, and therefore cease to feel like home. Secondly, the answer to where I'm from changes based on who's asking. Outside India, I introduce myself as Indian, or a resident of Mumbai. To a Mumbaikar, I 'come from' elsewhere. Even if I sidestep the question of language nativism, I 'come from' beyond the city's municipal limits. To people of a certain class, my suburb may as well be on another continent. Others know where it is, but they might raise their eyebrows and say, 'That's far!'

It is not 'far' as much as it is marginal. My location on the fringes makes me marginal in a microgeographic sense, as well as the emotional, social and political sense. The price of real estate, the religious and caste demographic decides whether or not we are deemed worthy of a clean and constant water supply, proper drainage, investments in culture and art. Over a million people live in the suburbs just beyond north Mumbai, but there is a woeful absence of public performance spaces and libraries. Bookstores rarely stock anything other than prescribed school textbooks. The marginality of a suburb can keep its residents in a state of limitation.

Questions of *where* you are from are therefore most often about *who* you are. I am defined by my genetic heritage, and by cultural, political and personal values, which in turn are shaped by my access to ideas outside of my geographic location. The more I read and travel, the more my location of 'self' changes.

As a child, I knew that the D type, C type, A type quarters in an industrial township were housing. Home was where my grandparents were. To my grandparents, home may have been their children, or ancestral homes, which bore memories of their own parents. When I first moved out and rented my own place like any twenty-something – with a mattress and a suitcase and little else – I was pleased. I felt grown up. But I was aware that this was temporary. A foothold. Less, a toehold. Home was still family, the one I had, or potentially, a future location with a new emotional anchor.

The heart is therefore always a compass for home. But the heart does not pull towards a few hundred square foot of real estate. Caves can be homes. Tents are homes, and not just for refugees. Communities like the nomadic Mongols have lived in tents for millennia. However temporary, home signals emotional tenure. As much as it is shelter and welcome, it is where you want to return.

Return is not always possible, though. When my brother and I returned to Lucknow after college, one of the first things we did was revisit a streetside eatery called Rover's. Our college-going aunts had taken us there for burgers and ice cream, which we ate sitting on a moped or a cycle rickshaw. It was among my happiest memories. But Rover's was no longer the same. The elderly man who served us was gone. The burgers were different. We'd tasted better ice cream in bigger cities. The sense of home contained in the memory of that place was irrecoverable.

Another great determinant of home is whether, and how, you are seen in public. Are you greeted? Do people *see* you at all?

On the street where I currently live, I recognise a number of people, even if I do not know their names. I know the vegetable guy, the grocery store family and their boys who deliver the goods to our doorstep, the guy who sells bananas, the pharmacy guy, the old man who squats on the ground with a basket of plums and strawberries, the woman who alters clothes, the auto-rickshaw drivers parked at the building's gates. I have watched them go grey.

I buy bananas even if I do not want them, if I catch the eye of the regular vendor. I guiltily sneak past the regular vegetable seller if I happen to have bought tomatoes at another stall that had redder, plumper produce.

The regular auto drivers don't know my name, but they are unlikely to turn me away if I have somewhere to go in a hurry. If one of them disappears for weeks, I wonder what's happened, and if I see one after a long absence, I say nothing but I think to myself: *Long time!* I know that when I'm gone for months, they must be thinking the same.

In this witnessing and recognition, our lives are contained as much as they are contained in passports and rent agreements. When I move houses or cities, I lose this thread that binds me to my street and leads to a softening of the inner armour.

The cobbler at the end of the street, the surly tailor, the grocer – they lend me stability. The knowledge that someone is around, doing valuable and timeless work, allows me to feel as if some version of me has also been here forever: a woman with a broken sandal; a woman craving a new dress; a woman who can set up a tailoring shop in hard times.

When public space changes dramatically – a park is turned into apartment blocks, a cinema turns into a shopping mall filled with expensive brands, a slum is demolished and its residents scattered – it can cause an alienation as sharp as moving to another city. Since it is politics that determines access to public space and services, to be cut off from the political process through being stripped of voting rights or being denied the right to contest elections, also translates into a denial of home, and the safety and freedom it represents.

*

Sometimes I think of home as morning mist. I see it as wispy strands engulfing everything around me. I feel its cool fingers on my face, but it is beyond my grasp.

They say, at moments when you think you might lose it, your life flashes through your mind as a set of images. This is also how I think of home – as a moving picture rather than a still life. Names of places and rivers. Trains, sugarcane fields, mustard fields, dacoits and gangs, hills, skyscrapers, and a very flat horizon. Heads of corn on burning coals, mounds of groundnut slow-roasting on a foggy winter evening, hand-carts, a certain grace of manner, headstones. Men and women dressed in a single piece of fabric. A basket of fish. Weighing scales that have remained more or less unchanged over four thousand years. Pebbles substituted for standard weight measures, and my willingness to accept that the pebble weights are accurate.

Like mist, these things disappear. Rivers and hills too may disappear within my own lifetime. But like a train of thought, like a film of moving images, something of home remains within.

This too is a way to define home – as that which we have lived and that which will not leave us: the love that will not quit on us, our social habits, our sources of self-esteem, hunger, shame, genes, fragments of solidarity, refuge, and undisturbed rest.

# ACKNOWLEDGEMENTS

This book draws upon memory, my own but also those of my family members, so I must begin by thanking the family for the stories I've been told, and for maintaining the physical sites that offer a sense of place in our various ancestral homes.

I owe my mother, Yasmin Zaidi, all kinds of thanks for the wonderful, intricate work she has done on the illustrations accompanying this book. And for everything else, including building that home within the ancestral home, and her stubborn faith that it matters.

Several conversations with friends, acquaintances and strangers helped me think through my ideas about home and homeland. For conversation, hospitality, book recommendations, caffeine, sweets and savouries, I must thank Kavita Srivastav, Rajeev Yadav, Rima Hooja, Alok Rai, Abhishek and Mamta Pandey, Ramesh Dixit, Naseeruddin Sanjari, Lenin Maududi (a pseudonym), Ali Khan Mahmudabad, Riaz Tehsin, and for clarifying some questions of law, Gautam Bhatia. I am grateful to Om Thanvi, Apurva Narain, Fatima Rizvi, Rahul Soni, Saeed Naqvi, for helping me chase an elusive reference.

I owe a debt of gratitude to Salman Khan and his father, Zishan Khan, for helping with the transcription of my grandfather's literary memoir.

I owe another debt to Saka Ram Garāsia, for his guidance and time, without which I could not have managed a significant part of my research in such a short period of time. I recall with affection the schoolteachers in Sirohi and former schoolmates who met me with kindness and warmth upon my return.

It has been a pleasure working with my editor Chris Harrison, and the wonderful team at Cambridge University Press and Riot.

I was immensely lucky in winning the Nine Dots Prize, and am grateful for the support I've received from the Kadas Prize

Foundation. Professor Simon Goldhill and Professor David Runciman were kind enough to read an early draft and gave valuable feedback. Double thanks are due to Jane Tinkler, for various conversations during the course of making this book, but especially for helping me access a document that was impossible to find in India.

I am also grateful for my time at the Centre for Research in the Arts, Social Sciences and Humanities, Cambridge University, for giving me an opportunity to read, access some wonderful libraries and attend intellectually stimulating seminars that helped me connect some of the dots and make sense of this fragile thing called home.

# NOTES

## Chapter 1

1. www.lexico.com/en/definition/bigha.
2. Raziya Tehsin, *Shikari, Shikar, Jangal se Pyar* (Hindi) (Praveen Prakashan, 2012), page 58.
3. Rima Hooja, *Rajasthan: A Concise History* (Rupa Publications India, 2018), page 723.
4. Ibid., page 710.
5. www.jklakshmicement.com/wp-content/uploads/2019/01/JKLCL-Web-Upload-Sustainability-Report-2014–16.pdf
6. www.indiaenvironmentportal.org.in/files/file/Draft%20Mineral%20Policy%202015.pdf
7. https://ibm.gov.in/writereaddata/files/10072016165142Lakshmi%20Cement_1_3_16.pdf
8. https://caravanmagazine.in/politics/ready-for-the-struggle-for-bhil-pradesh-bharatiya-tribal-party
9. http://udaipurtimes.com/live-in-a-jaw-dropping-news-about-the-tribes/
10. https://caravanmagazine.in/politics/ready-for-the-struggle-for-bhil-pradesh-bharatiya-tribal-party
11. www.ssoar.info/ssoar/bitstream/handle/document/42201/ssoar-2011-singh_negi_et_al-Development_projects_vs_internally_displaced.pdf?sequence=1
12. Chinmay Tumbe, *India Moving: A History of Migration* (Penguin Viking, 2018), page 197.
13. www.indiaspend.com/as-sc-hearing-nears-adivasis-recall-evictions-that-led-to-forest-law/
14. www.newsclick.in/first-fired-upon-now-criminal-cases-registered-against-tribals-madhya-pradesh
15. https://indianexpress.com/article/india/upper-caste-hindus-richest-in-india-own-41-total-assets-says-study-on-wealth-distri

bution-5582984/?fbclid=IwAR3cHbJJxyWerN4N9hdjrjPKr2-
sOqdf7SNa32myOztW_-OKsrfcxj4PANM

16. www.telegraphindia.com/india/homeless-in-city-of-birth-
3-out-of-5-indians-without-roof-not-migrants/cid/1710779?
fbclid=IwAR1vwDUcZ7XoJyCDmMFuHWD_Uj6EpwrFrt3z
MgYyo3Ghoirnp7eKwK6hwrI

17. https://theprint.in/india/every-second-st-every-third-dalit-
muslim-in-india-poor-not-just-financially-un-report/262270/?
fbclid=IwAR2cOj51wzyyhJDtUn6Fu0VFddsK_06NrEhqA6BT
kp7lxP-Nv7jD4kSk_zg

18. www.newsclick.in/tribals-rajasthan-banswara-forced-mort
gage-children-earn-livelihood

## Chapter 2

1. Respective translation of occupational caste names
mentioned: tailors, butchers, oil pressers, removers of
waste/cleaners, washermen, Mughals, singers/itinerant
traders, carpenters, drummers, vegetable sellers,
performers (often rope-walk artists).

2. Roger Jeffery and Jens Lerche (eds.), *Social and Political Change
in Uttar Pradesh: European Perspectives* (Manohar Books, 2003),
page 18.

3. Venkitesh Ramakrishnan (ed.), *Uttar Pradesh: The Road Ahead*
(Academic Foundation, 2009), page 73.

4. www.csas.ed.ac.uk/mutiny/Texts-Part2.html

5. www.thenational.ae/world/in-pictures-uttar-pradesh-gains-
reputation-as-india-s-failed-state-1.256442

6. http://ncrb.gov.in/

7. https://archive.indiaspend.com/cover-story/lies-and-statistics
-how-indias-most-populous-state-fudges-crime-data-11091

8. www.hindustantimes.com/india-news/india-has-33-69-lakh
-gun-licences-uttar-pradesh-tops-list-with-12-77-lakh/story-
uRQ9XGCy9wpczOiEMcFmAN.html

9. Mrinal Pande, *The Other Country: Dispatches from the Mofussil*
(Penguin India, 2011), page 190.

10. www.livemint.com/Politics/49glAPNZcuYLvTMI6L4tiK/
Uttar-Pradesh-the-land-of-la-tamancha.html

11. www.indiatoday.in/magazine/special-report/story/
20141020-guns-dhar-madhya-pradesh-illegal-firearms-
indore-805479-2014-10-09

12. www.thenational.ae/opinion/comment/gun-law-the-unstoppable-rise-of-indian-police-encounter-shootings-1.811634

13. www.patrika.com/meerut-news/west-up-has-its-own-histry-of-gang-war-have-lost-many-lives-3076512/

14. www.outlookindia.com/magazine/story/a-slice-of-sicily/229602

15. https://economictimes.indiatimes.com/news/politics-and-nation/call-him-bahubali-at-your-own-risk/articleshow/57443344.cms?from=mdr

16. www.thelallantop.com/up-election/story-of-mafia-gangs-of-up-which-comprised-of-virendra-pratap-shahi-harishankar-tiwari-mokhtar-ansari/

17. www.outlookindia.com/website/story/the-gunda-of-kunda/218953

18. www.rediff.com/election/2002/feb/14_upr_bash_rep_1.htm

19. http://timesofindia.indiatimes.com/articleshow/11075499.cms?utm_source=contentofinterest&utm_medium=text&utm_campaign=cppst

20. https://daily.bhaskar.com/news/UP-photos-robinhoods-who-scare-worlds-most-wanted-dawood-ibrahim-3540419.html

21. www.indiaspend.com/indian-police-forces-short-of-communications-transport-weapons-but-not-money/

22. Manoj Singh, *Yogi Adityanath* (Neelkanth Prakashan, 2018), page 31.

23. www.inuth.com/india/politics/heres-the-few-crime-records-of-ups-next-cm-yogi-adityanath/

24. http://archive.asianage.com/india/chhota-rajan-also-gets-sharpshooters-865

25. www.dnaindia.com/india/report-the-fall-of-the-underworld-2289694

26. https://thewire.in/157299/police-ips-criminality-mumbai-underworld/

27. http://services.iriskf.org/data/articles/Document116112005142.709597E-02.pdf

28. www.india-seminar.com/1999/483/483%20rai.htm

29. www.business-standard.com/article/current-affairs/most-police-believe-muslims-and-dalits-more-prone-to-commit-crimes-119090800708_1.html

30. https://indianexpress.com/article/india/politics/amit-shah-calls-azamgarh-the-base-of-terrorists/

31. www.indiatoday.in/elections/lok-sabha-2019/story/samaj
    wadi-party-turned-azamgarh-into-stronghold-of-terrorism-
    yogi-adityanath-1510162-2019-04-25
32. https://sangeetnatak.gov.in/sna/citation_popup.php?id=1706
    &at=5
33. www.indiatoday.in/india/north/story/even-god-cannot-
    stop-crimes-in-up-durga-prasad-yadav-uttar-pradesh-
    samajwadi-party-101469-2012-05-08

# Chapter 3

1. www.theguardian.com/books/2014/jun/01/maya-angelou-
   appreciation-afua-hirsch
2. https://gulfnews.com/world/asia/india/census-more-than
   -19500-languages-spoken-in-india-as-mother-tongues-1
   .2244791
3. https://mhrd.gov.in/language-education
4. http://censusindia.gov.in/Census_Data_2001/Census_
   Data_Online/Language/Statement1.aspx
5. www.dailyo.in/voices/imposition-of-hindi-belt-politics-
   regional-languages-braj-urdu-malayalam-english/story/1/
   18271.html?fbclid=IwAR136N8xcdh78a1wDDPcAEqAiaxrEp-
   x5dOFpUpbJNSdbUyuV1fcIy8t5mM
6. Alok Rai, *Hindi Nationalism* (Orient Blackswan, 2001), page
   117.
7. www.news18.com/news/india/non-hindi-states-come-
   together-to-protest-against-hindi-imposition-1461931.html
8. www.hindustantimes.com/india-news/anti-hindi-
   movement-re-surfaces-in-bengal-leader-says-bjp-s-rise-
   a-threat-to-regional-languages/story-
   waqTnAfUTHrNyqKmZyPw8N.html
9. https://caravanmagazine.in/culture/gond-gondi-koitur-
   dictionary-adivasi
10. www.thehindu.com/thread/arts-culture-society/india-
    a-land-of-many-tongues/article19445187.ece
11. www.downtoearth.org.in/interviews/language-is-the-only-
    tool-for-expressing-identity-and-culture-46695
12. www.hindustantimes.com/dehradun/sanskrit-now-
    compulsory-for-even-class-1-2-students-in-uttarakhand
    /story-FOyvvFUoJXCibFYpSUgfxM.html

13. http://censusindia.gov.in/2011Census/C-16_25062018_NEW
    .pdf
14. Rai, *Hindi Nationalism*, page 102.
15. Ibid., page 8.
16. Ibid., page 69.
17. Ibid., page 110.
18. Ibid., page 102.
19. Vibhuti Narain Rai, *Sampradayik Dange aur Bharatiya Police* (Radhakrishan Prakashan, 2016), pages 64–65.
20. https://indianexpress.com/article/india/speaking-sanskrit-keeps-diabetes-cholesterol-in-control-bjp-mp-says-in-lok-sabha-6164057/?fbclid=IwAR0FSELW2KF9v5trV7qnRT8V-IZ4uvECQAlTl3faG626setsjqR6ShezrEY
21. www.epw.in/system/files/pdf/1961_13/15/sanskritisation.pdf
22. www.downtoearth.org.in/blog/water/saraswati-river-myth-or-mirage-62726
23. Tony Joseph, *Early Indians: The Story of Our Ancestors and Where We Came From* (Juggernaut, 2018), page 224.
24. https://thewire.in/the-sciences/the-saraswati-is-a-river-that-never-was-and-flowed-always-in-the-peoples-hearts
25. www.thequint.com/news/india/searching-for-saraswati-documentary-review-nyt-op-docs-project
26. www.huffpost.com/entry/is-sanskrit-indispensable-for-hindu-litrugy_b_1956033
27. *Manusmriti*, trans. G. Bühler, https://archive.org/details/ManuSmriti_201601, https://archive.org/details/manusmriti_201607
28. *Dharmasutras: The Law Codes of Ancient India*, trans. Patrick Olivelle (Oxford World's Classics, 1999).
29. www.business-standard.com/article/current-affairs/income-inequality-in-india-top-10-upper-caste-households-own-60-wealth-119011400105_1.html
30. www.scmp.com/news/asia/south-asia/article/2024566/indias-dalits-refuse-bury-cow-carcasses-escalating-protests
31. www.bbc.com/news/world-asia-india-43581122
32. www.news18.com/news/india/up-students-refuse-mid-day-meal-prepared-by-lower-caste-cook-school-throws-out-food-after-protest-1871653.html

33. www.academia.edu/11562065/Caste_Discrimination_ in_Mid_day_meals_MDM_
34. https://theconversation.com/hinduism-and-its-complicated-history-with-cows-and-people-who-eat-them-80586
35. https://scroll.in/latest/924811/jharkhand-adivasi-professor-arrested-for-2017-facebook-post-on-right-to-eat-beef-huffpost-india
36. www.indiatoday.in/india/story/pehlu-khan-lynching-rajasthan-alwar-court-accused-acquitted-1580945-2019-08-14
37. https://caravanmagazine.in/caste/what-hindi-keeps-hidden? fbclid=IwAR2GDEEBn5dHjcAB2Vy5gIm_pEdeQtSlBy11366Y mj4LxQ2SSNwLTqDtz4o
38. https://scroll.in/article/737715/fact-check-india-wasnt-the-first-place-sanskrit-was-recorded-it-was-syria?fbclid= IwAR2oy2rRqyUhTOoj9_5ij-0zka9OtjVrHBrl-EnRwAmsYxhMPR-rVDQ7PB8
39. www.thehindu.com/news/cities/Delhi/Artists-reclaim-DJB-wall-in-Shahdara-with-Urdu-couplet/article14513848.ece#
40. https://thewire.in/communalism/panjab-university-moots-proposal-to-group-urdu-with-foreign-languages
41. https://thediplomat.com/2019/07/indias-war-on-urdu/? fbclid=IwAR2B76vETiBLqcuxQvysmmLkMoMkJbANU1B_E e4MpE5fR0BvTlIVKmwDl9w
42. www.thehindu.com/news/national/other-states/bsp-corporator-takes-oath-in-urdu-is-charged-with-intent-to-hurt-religious-sentiments/article21665609.ece
43. http://censusindia.gov.in/Census_And_You/religion.aspx
44. https://twitter.com/sowmyarao_/status/701813753742884864/ photo/1?ref_src=twsrc%5Etfw%7Ctwcamp%5Etweetembed% 7Ctwterm%5E701813753742884864&ref_url=https%3A%2F% 2Fwww.rvcj.com%2Fperson-reading-urdu-book-metro-some thing-happened-will-traumatize%2F
45. http://censusindia.gov.in/Census_And_You/religion.aspx
46. www.livemint.com/mint-lounge/features/-poetry-will-be-turmeric-caught-in-the-cracks-1564746117022.html
47. https://scroll.in/article/930416/i-am-miya-why-poetry-by-bengal-origin-muslims-in-their-mother-tongue-is-shaking-up-assam

48. www.firstpost.com/india/what-hiren-gohains-bitter-criticism-of-miyah-poetry-tells-us-about-assamese-nationalism-6931041.html

## Chapter 4

1. Tumbe, *India Moving*, page 230.
2. Sujata Anandan, *Samrat: How the Shiv Sena Changed Mumbai Forever* (HarperCollins India, 2014), page 54.
3. Tumbe, *India Moving*, page 220.
4. Anandan, *Samrat*, page 60.
5. Ibid., pages 195–96.
6. https://qz.com/india/717519/the-worlds-biggest-survey-of-slums-is-underway-in-india/
7. http://censusindia.gov.in/Census_And_You/migrations.aspx
8. Tumbe, *India Moving*, page 115.
9. Badri Narayan, *Culture and Emotional Economy of Migration* (Routledge South Asia, 2019), page 10.
10. www.undp.org/content/dam/india/docs/india_urban_poverty_report_2009_related.pdf
11. http://mohua.gov.in/upload/uploadfiles/files/1566.pdf
12. www.lausanne.org/content/lga/2012–11/people-and-their-religions-on-the-move-challenge-and-opportunities-of-international-migration
13. Narayan, *Culture and Emotional Economy*, page 71.
14. Ibid., page 3.
15. Ibid., page 63.
16. www.pewresearch.org/fact-tank/2017/03/03/india-is-a-top-source-and-destination-for-worlds-migrants/ft_17–03-03_indiamigration_remittance/
17. www.sbs.com.au/yourlanguage/hindi/en/article/2019/07/24/india-working-enabling-nris-vote-elections
18. https://sarai.net/the-quest-for-bodoland-social-media-in-the-time-of-a-separatist-movement-part-one/
19. www.bbc.com/news/world-asia-india-48754802
20. https://scroll.in/latest/888676/assam-former-presidents-family-members-among-40-lakh-people-excluded-from-final-nrc-draft
21. https://thewire.in/rights/assam-nrc-reverification-prateek-hajela

22. https://economictimes.indiatimes.com/news/politics-and-nation/bjp-to-tell-sc-it-rejects-nrc-says-assam-minister-sarma/articleshow/71268958.cms
23. www.indiatoday.in/india/story/amit-shah-nrc-speech-kolkata-bjp-elections-citizenship-illegal-immigrants-1605194-2019-10-01
24. www.bbc.com/news/world-asia-india-45192701
25. www.indiatoday.in/india/story/citizenship-amendment-bill-all-you-need-to-know-about-cab-1627516-2019-12-11
26. www.reuters.com/article/india-election-speech/amit-shah-vows-to-throw-illegal-immigrants-into-bay-of-bengal-idUSKCN1RO1YD

## Chapter 5

1. https://theconversation.com/tampering-with-history-how-indias-ruling-party-is-erasing-the-muslim-heritage-of-the-nations-cities-116160
2. Mizra Ghalib in *The Last Bungalow: Writings on Allahabad*, ed. Arvind Krishna Mehrotra (Penguin India, 2007), page 47.
3. Mehrotra, *Last Bungalow*, page 2.
4. Ibid., pages 84–86.
5. Ibid., page 313.
6. Neelum Saran Gour, *Three Rivers and a Tree* (Rupa Publications India, 2015), page 24.
7. Ibid., page 111.
8. Ibid., page 117.
9. Ibid., page 86.
10. Ibid., pages 241–43.
11. www.hindustantimes.com/india-news/allahabad-university-hostels-raided-crude-bombs-and-raw-material-recovered/story-tjHMDRvjySJkaidyLyco5M.html
12. www.thehindu.com/news/national/other-states/dalit-professor-issued-notice-for-comment-on-hindu-deity/article29310481.ece
13. Svetlana Boym, *The Future of Nostalgia* (Basic Books, 2002), page xvi.
14. Mehrotra (ed.), *Last Bungalow*, page 314.
15. Rai, *Hindi Nationalism*, page 11.

16. www.theguardian.com/cities/2019/mar/28/kumbh-mela-cleaning-up-after-the-worlds-largest-human-gathering; www.downtoearth.org.in/news/pollution/faith-to-filth-thanks-to-kumbh-prayagraj-sinks-in-solid-waste-64579; https://thewire.in/environment/allahabad-ngt-kumbh-mela
17. www.livemint.com/news/india/four-separate-pleas-seeking-review-of-ayodhya-verdict-filed-in-supreme-court-1157 5636086334.html
18. https://thewire.in/communalism/kashi-mathura-baaki-hain-why-the-ayodhya-verdict-wont-offer-any-respite-from-saffron-hatred
19. https://thewire.in/society/junaids-lynching-and-the-making-of-a-new-india-beyond-recognition
20. https://scroll.in/latest/932542/delhi-bjp-mps-claims-on-illegal-mosques-are-false-says-fact-finding-team

## Chapter 6

1. www.indiatoday.in/india/east/story/bjp-leader-giriraj-singh-says-those-opposing-modi-will-have-to-go-to-pak-189678 –2014-04–19
2. www.asianage.com/india/politics/250319/people-who-want-to-lecture-on-secularism-can-go-to-pakistan-uma-bharti.html
3. www.business-standard.com/article/news-ians/go-to-pakistan-if-you-want-to-celebrate-it-goa-cm-119050301173_1.html
4. www.ndtv.com/india-news/those-opposing-article-370-move-should-go-to-pakistan-union-minister-ramdas-athawale-2092048
5. www.thenewsminute.com/article/bjp-mp-calls-ex-ias-officer-traitor-criticising-union-government-108625
6. Tumbe, *India Moving*, page 163.
7. Ibid., page 176.
8. Ibid., page 170.
9. https://thewire.in/history/alwars-long-history-hindutva-casts-shadow-even-today
10. www.aljazeera.com/news/2017/11/forgotten-massacre-ignited-kashmir-dispute-171106144526930.html
11. Attia Hosain, *Sunlight on a Broken Column* (1961; Penguin Random House India, 2009), page 287.

12. Saeed Naqvi, *Being the Other: The Muslim in India* (Aleph Book Company, 2016), page 23.
13. Maulana Abul Kalam Azad, *India Wins Freedom* (Orient Blackswan, 1988), pages 226–27.
14. Ibid., page 216.
15. Seema Mustafa, *Azadi's Daughter: Being a Secular Muslim in India: A Memoir* (Speaking Tiger, 2017), pages 102–03.
16. Naqvi, *Being the Other*, page 101.
17. https://theprint.in/india/governance/muslim-school-kids-called-names-and-told-to-go-to-pakistan-mothers-blame-tv-hate/200701/
18. https://indianexpress.com/article/cities/delhi/go-to-pakistan-20-25-men-barge-into-gurgaon-home-assault-family-5638962/
19. www.news18.com/news/politics/man-shot-at-in-bihars-begusarai-for-muslim-name-as-attacker-shouts-go-to-pakistan-owaisi-says-community-now-target-practice-2161239.html
20. Azad, *India Wins Freedom*, page 247.
21. https://eurasiafuture.com/2019/04/06/modis-global-danger-akhand-bharat-is-the-lebensraum-of-the-21st-century/
22. www.thecitizen.in/index.php/en/NewsDetail/index/4/17377/Kashmir-Two-Words-Union-Territory-Says-It-All
23. www.minorityaffairs.gov.in/sites/default/files/sachar_comm.pdf
24. https://scroll.in/article/809187/why-india-must-end-the-states-amnesia-about-the-horrors-that-accompanied-partition
25. Joseph, *Early Indians*, page 212.
26. www.unicef.org/media/files/Child_Marriage_Report_7_17_LR.pdf
27. www.girlsnotbrides.org/child-marriage/india/
28. www.indiatoday.in/india/story/child-marriage-will-put-an-end-to-love-jihad-says-bjp-mla-gopal-parmar-1227492-2018-05-06
29. www.naidunia.com/chhattisgarh/bilaspur-love-jihad-case-hearing-in-chhattisgarh-high-court-in-a-plea-to-declare-marriage-void-3143326
30. www.indiatoday.in/india/story/bjp-mla-rajesh-misra-daughter-sakshi-video-honour-killing-dalit-marriage-1566358-2019-07-10

31. https://frontline.thehindu.com/static/html/fl2325/stories/20061229001810100.htm
32. www.thehindu.com/news/national/other-states/hindu-yuva-vahini-members-barge-into-house-beat-up-muslim-man-girlfriend/article17952482.ece
33. www.aljazeera.com/news/2016/12/india-sees-huge-spike-honour-killings-161207153333597.html
34. www.thehindu.com/data/the-many-shades-of-rape-cases-in-delhi/article6261042.ece
35. https://thewire.in/featured/prashant-bhushan-and-the-impiety-of-the-pious
36. Hooja, *Rajasthan*, page 370.
37. File no. 108-P (Secret) of 1946, Government of India, Political Department
38. www.outlookindia.com/newswire/story/jodha-akbar-controversy-reaches-supreme-court/550258

## Chapter 7

1. www.livemint.com/Politics/mnVzCfIEbqvzEu01LTxqLM/Urban-Indians-still-get-married-the-way-their-grandparents-d.html
2. www.youtube.com/watch?v=uD5Pe4k3myI
3. www.epw.in/journal/2000/14/commentary/bengali-widows-varanasi.html
4. www.washingtonpost.com/archive/politics/1992/09/25/the-widows-chant/b7a7481f-1d1e-4943-b219-c995bd427ce7/
5. www.downtoearth.org.in/news/health/selective-abortions-killed-22–5-million-female-foetuses-in-china-india-64043
6. https://journals.plos.org/plosone/article?id=10.1371/journal.pone.0107172
7. www.thehindubusinessline.com/specials/india-interior/are-boys-fed-better-than-girls/article8566303.ece
8. www.livemint.com/Politics/dWUqT4epdPTHNAYuKYVThK/No-vegetarianism-is-not-growing-in-India.html
9. www.edexlive.com/live-story/2017/oct/01/archaic-system-in-bhu-ensures-that-only-boys-have-all-the-fun-female-residents-imposed-with-biased-r-1242.html
10. Tumbe, *India Moving*, page 14.
11. www.unodc.org/documents/data-and-analysis/GSH2018/GSH18_Gender-related_killing_of_women_and_girls.pdf

12. www.oxfamindia.org/sites/default/files/2018-10/WP-Measurement-of-Domestic-Violence-in-National-Family-Health-Survey-surveys-and-Some-Evidence-EN.pdf
13. https://kathmandupost.com/national/2019/03/07/debate-over-nepali-womens-right-to-pass-on-citizenship-to-children-reignites-as-house-committee-holds-discussions-on-controversial-provisions
14. https://thewire.in/rights/women-without-parents-an-nrc-ground-report

## Chapter 8

1. blogs.harvard.edu
2. Madho Lal Hussein, *Verses of a Lowly Fakir*, trans. Naveed Alam (Penguin India, 2016), verse 52.
3. www.livemint.com/Opinion/83aeFFG0sv4NkWsd4zJdoN/Wali-vs-Modi-the-tale-of-two-poets.html
4. www.news18.com/news/india/varaun-bahar-singer-of-controversial-bhejo-kabristan-song-arrested-in-ups-gonda-2246467.html
5. www.thequint.com/state-elections-2017/uttar-pradesh-elections-2017/kabristan-shamshan-comment-muslim-voters-up
6. https://hindi.indiatvnews.com/video/politics/send-sp-and-bsp-to-kabristan-and-choose-a-govt-which-will-bring-development-in-state-yogi-adityanath-506530
7. https://thewire.in/politics/bjp-up-election-strategies
8. Panchanan Mitra, *Prehistoric India* (1927; Gyan Publishing, 2010), ch. 14.
9. Nagendra K. Singh (ed.), *Ritualistic Philosophy of Death and Disposal of the Dead* (Global Vision, 2004).
10. Joseph, *Early Indians*, page 177.
11. Jonathan Parry, *Death in Banaras* (Cambridge University Press, 1994), pages 184–85.
12. www.livemint.com/Leisure/3NPybJyH0d04sqXine2CCK/Six-feet-under.html
13. www.outlookindia.com/magazine/story/a-flame-beneath-the-ground/298344
14. Danesh A. Chekki, *Religion and Social System of the Vīraśaiva Community* (Greenwood, 1997).

15. www.outlookindia.com/magazine/story/a-flame-beneath-the-ground/298344
16. K. S. Singh (gen. ed.), *People of India: Maharashtra*, part 3, volume XXX (Popular Prakashan, 2004).
17. Joanna Pfaff-Czarnecka and Gerard Toffin (eds.), *The Politics of Belonging in the Himalayas* (Sage Publishing, 2011).
18. K. S. Singh (gen. ed.), *People of India: Maharashtra*, part 2, volume XXX (Popular Prakashan, 2004).
19. Sukhvir Singh Gahlot and Banshi Dhar, *Castes and Tribes of Rajasthan* (Jain Brothers, 1989).
20. Veena Bhasin, 'Habitat, Economy and Society: The Kathodis of Rajasthan', *Journal of Human Ecology*, volume 14, issue 1, 2003; http://krepublishers.com/02-Journals/JHE/JHE-14-0-000-000-2003-Web/JHE-14-1-001-03-Abst-PDF/JHE-14-1-001-03-Bhasin-V/JHE-14-1-001-03-Bhasin-V-Tt.pdf
21. https://qz.com/india/956445/hindu-by-birth-muslim-by-wisdom-the-roots-of-yogi-adityanaths-cult-group/
22. www.news18.com/news/india/turned-away-from-crematorium-mp-dalit-family-performs-last-rites-of-kin-in-front-of-home-1613859.html
23. www.ndtv.com/tamil-nadu-news/denied-road-to-cremation-ground-dalits-dump-body-from-tamil-nadu-bridge-2088789
24. www.bbc.com/news/world-south-asia-11229170
25. www.rediff.com/news/2003/mar/06bihar.htm
26. https://indianexpress.com/article/cities/delhi/grave-concerns-5024790/
27. Naqvi, *Being the Other*, pages 126–27.
28. Parry, *Death in Banaras*, pages 26–27.
29. Ibid., page 26.
30. https://scroll.in/article/926812/the-tragic-death-of-mohammed-shaikh-the-rickshaw-puller-who-bared-his-life-in-a-poignant-video?fbclid=IwAR3DXIbZZ0RIzRIcwPaPVTC1xKawaTIUkpJM_mkol8Yhf8UDuLWTiIL4uts
31. www.nytimes.com/2010/02/26/arts/design/26burial.html
32. www.theguardian.com/world/2017/aug/30/taj-mahal-muslim-tomb-not-hindu-temple-indian-court-told
33. www.aljazeera.com/news/2015/08/outspoken-indian-scholar-rationalist-killed-150830093019963.html

34. www.hindustantimes.com/lucknow/mentally-challenged-man-brings-hindus-muslims-together-even-in-death-in-up-s-moradabad/story-HiZlscQRbRp0Dznqs8Kc3I.html
35. www.thehindu.com/news/national/other-states/pm-modi-to-visit-kabirs-mausoleum-in-maghar-today/article 24277150.ece

## Chapter 9

1. Agyeya, *Ajneya Rachnawali: Vol 2*; pages 458–460 (Bhartiya Gyanpeeth 2011).
2. Translation mine.